WAITING FOR GOD

Simone Weil

WAITING FOR GOD

TRANSLATED BY EMMA CRAUFURD

With an Introduction by Leslie A. Fiedler

Harper & Row, Publishers, New York
Grand Rapids, Philadelphia, St. Louis, San Francisco
London, Singapore, Sydney, Tokyo, Toronto

This book was originally published by G. P. Putnam's Sons and is here reprinted by arrangement.

First HARPER COLOPHON edition published in 1973

INTERNATIONAL STANDARD BOOK NUMBER: 0–06–090295–7

96 97 98 99 RRD H 30

Contents

Biographical Note[*]

SIMONE WEIL was born in Paris on February 3, 1909. The house of her birth in the Boulevard de Strasbourg has since been pulled down to make room for the rue de Metz.

Thanks to her brother André, who was her elder by three years, she was exceptionally advanced in her knowledge of literature and science. At six she could quote passages of Racine by heart, and although her studies were constantly interrupted as a result of the First World War, she obtained her *baccalaureat es lettres* with distinction in June, 1924, at the age of fifteen. The president of the board of examiners, who was a specialist in the literature of the early Middle Ages, gave her 19 out of 20 after her oral test.

During her year of philosophy she worked under La Senne; then she had Alain † as her master for two years at the Collège Henri IV when she prepared for the competitive entrance examination of the *Ecole Normale*. Alain, who

---

* This note, provided by the French publishers, replaces the Introduction and notes by the Reverend J. M. Perrin, which are withdrawn at their request.

† Pseudonym of the well-known French philosopher and essayist, Emile Auguste Chartier (1868–).

recognized that she had philosophical genius and saw in her "a power of thought which was rare," followed her development with attentive and kindly interest, noting, however, that she had to be on her guard against too close reasoning expressed in almost impenetrable language and that, in the end, "she had been willing to turn from the deep abstract subtleties which were a game for her and to train herself in direct analysis."

She entered the *Ecole Normale Supérieure* in 1928, left as a qualified teacher of philosophy in 1931, and was appointed to the secondary school for girls at Le Puy. There, from December, 1931 until the spring of 1932 she gave public proof of her uncompromising opposition toward official compulsion of any sort helping and encouraging the unemployed workmen of the town by her marked sympathy and by taking direct action against the municipal authorities.

She had friends in the group of the *Révolution Prolétarienne*, and in 1932 she began to contribute to this review. She was thus given an opportunity of expressing in clear and accurate terms and with a real knowledge of human problems her main ideas and her feeling about the condition of the workers.

Appointed to a school at Auxerre in October, 1932, and in 1933 to one at Roanne, she then decided to take a year's leave so that she could experience fully the working people's life to which she had already tried to accustom herself by working in the fields of the Jura during the summer months.

Having taken a job in the Renault works, she hired a room in a neighboring house and strove, in spite of the headaches and delicate health she had always had to contend with, to avoid anything that could make her lot differ in the slightest degree from that of her companions in the workshop.

When her leave came to an end in 1935, she again took a teaching post, this time at the girls' secondary school at Bourges. She left in the summer of 1936 to go to Barcelona in the beginning of August. She wanted to be able to judge for herself of the struggle between the "Reds" and the "Francoites."

During the following October she returned to France after having shared the sufferings of the Republican Army for several weeks on the Catalonian front and having experienced in the very depths of her being the utter calamity of war.

Another period of leave, this time on account of illness, prevented her from taking up before 1937 an appointment at the secondary school for girls at Saint Quentin. Once more, in January, 1938, her health obliged her to stop working until the time when the Second World War broke out.

On June 13, 1940, she decided to leave Paris and settled at Marseilles in October of the same year, with her family.

In June, 1941, a friend introduced her to the Reverend Father Perrin, who was then at the Dominican Convent in Marseilles and who, two years later, was to be arrested by the Gestapo. Father Perrin introduced her to Gustave Thibon with whom she stayed for a while in Ardeche. There, once more impelled by her longing to share in a life of direct contact with the soil, she engaged in manual work, either in the fields during the harvest, or in the vineyards at the time of the grape-gathering. She did not on that account give up any of her studies of philosophy, whether Greek or

Hindu, and went on widening her knowledge of Sanskrit. At the same time her mystical tendencies and her preoccupation with the notion of God became more pronounced, leading her to write the pages on the Our Father and on the Love of God which are to be read farther on.

On returning to Marseilles for the winter she continued her talks and discussions with Father Perrin and at his request she expounded her thoughts on Plato and the Pythagoreans to the circle that used to meet in the crypt of the Dominican Convent there.

When Father Perrin was chosen as Superior at Montpellier, in March, 1942, he did not lose contact with Simone Weil. They went on meeting, writing letters, and exchanging their views right up to the time when Simone left France.

It was probably on May 15, 1942, that she wrote the long letter, which she calls her "spiritual autobiography," to Father Perrin, then away on a journey. Her boat left the port on May 17. She spent three weeks at Casablanca, in a camp where travelers in transit from France to America were confined. Here she prepared a certain number of additional papers. These she sent to Father Perrin as a spiritual legacy, and on May 26, in a last letter of farewell, she completed and added to that of May 15.

Soon after reaching New York at the end of June, 1942, she received a call to serve under the French provisional government and left for England on November 10.

In London she was commissioned to make a study of official documents; she outlined plans and wrote a long memorandum on the rights and duties, either reciprocal or united, of the State and the individual.* She wanted to share the hardship of those she had left in France and carried this to such a point that, although overtired and run down, she refused the extra nourishment ordered by the doctors and kept strictly to the rations to which her compatriots in the occupied zone were limited at that time.

The state of her health became so much worse that, in the second fortnight of April, 1943, she was admitted to the Middlesex Hospital, whence she was transferred in the middle of August to a sanatorium at Ashford in Kent.

The last sentence she wrote in the notebook found after her death was: "The most important part of education—to teach the meaning of *to know* (in the scientific sense)."

The whole of Simone Weil is contained in these few words.

A day or two later, on August 29, 1943, she died at Ashford.

The correspondence here published and the essays which follow were all sent or given to the Reverend Father Perrin by Simone Weil, at the time when she was still able to communicate with him.

In giving this collection of letters and essays the title of WAITING FOR GOD, the publisher has sought to suggest a favorite thought of Simone Weil which she expressed in the Greek words ἐν ὑπομένῃ: waiting in patience.

---

* Published as *L'Enracinement* (Gallimard, Paris, 1949). Eng. trans.: *The Need for Roots* (G. P. Putnam's Sons, New York, 1952).

WAITING FOR GOD

Introduction

SINCE HER DEATH, Simone Weil has come to seem more and more a special exemplar of sanctity for our time—the Outsider as Saint in an age of alienation, our kind of saint. In eight scant years, this young Frenchwoman, whom scarcely anyone had heard of before her sacrificial death in exile at the age of 34, has come to possess the imagination of many in the Western world. Catholic and Protestant, Christian and Jew, agnostic and devout, we have all turned to her with the profound conviction that the meaning of her experience is our meaning, that she is really *ours*. Few of us, to be sure, would find nothing to dissent from in her religious thought; fewer still would be capable of emulating the terrible purity of her life; none could measure himself, without shame, against the absolute ethos toward which she aspired. And yet she does not seem strange to us, as other mystics and witnesses of God have seemed strange; for though on one side her life touches the remote mysteries of the Divine Encounter, on the other it is rooted in a world with which we are familiar.

She speaks of the problems of belief in the vocabulary of

the unbeliever, of the doctrines of the Church in the words of the unchurched. The *askesis*, the "dark night of the soul," through which she passed to certitude, is the modern intellectual's familiar pattern of attraction toward and disillusionment with Marxism, the discipline of contemporary politics. The day-to-day struggles of trade unionism, unemployment, the Civil War in Spain, the role of the Soviet Union, anarchism, and pacifism—these are the determinants of her ideas, the unforeseen roads that led her to sanctity. Though she passed finally beyond politics, her thought bears to the end the mark of her early interests, as the teaching of St. Paul is influenced by his Rabbinical schooling, or that of St. Augustine by his training in rhetoric.

Before her death, scarcely any of Simone Weil's religious writings had been published. To those in France who thought of her still, in terms of her early political essays, as a somewhat unorthodox Marxist moving toward anarchism, the posthumous Christian books must have come as a shock. Surely, no "friend of God" in all history, had moved more unwillingly toward the mystic encounter. There is in her earlier work no sense of a groping toward the divine, no promise of holiness, no pursuit of a purity beyond this world —only a conventionally left-wing concern with the problems of industrialization, rendered in a tone at once extraordinarily inflexible and wonderfully sensitive.

The particular note of conviction in Simone Weil's testimony arises from the feeling that her role as a mystic was so *unintended*, one for which she had not in any sense prepared. An undertone of incredulity persists beneath her astonishing honesty: quite suddenly God had taken her, radical, agnostic, contemptuous of religious life and practice as she had observed it! She clung always to her sense of being an Outsider among the religious, to a feeling that her improbable approach had given her a special vocation, as an "apostle to the Gentiles," planted at "the intersection of Christianity and everything that is not Christianity." She refused to become, in the typical compensatory excess of the convert, more of the Church than those born into it; she would not even be baptized, and it is her unique position, at once in and out of institutionalized Catholicism, that determines her special role and meaning.

To those who consider themselves on the safe side of belief, she teaches the uncomfortable truth that the unbelief of many atheists is closer to a true love of God and a true sense of his nature, than the kind of easy faith which, never having *experienced* God, hangs a label bearing his name on some childish fantasy or projection of the ego. Like Kierkegaard, she preached the paradox of its being easier for a non-Christian to become a Christian, than for a "Christian" to become one. To those who believe in a single Revelation, and enjoy the warm sensation of being saved in a cozy circle of friends, she expounded the doctrine of a gospel spread in many "languages," of a divine Word shared among rival myths, in each of which certain important truths, implicit elsewhere, are made explicit. For those to whom religion means comfort and peace of mind, she brings the terrible reminder that Christ promised not peace but the sword, and that his own last words were a cry of absolute despair, the "*Eli, Eli, lama sabachthani!*" which is the true glory of Christianity.

But she always considered that her chief mission was to those still "submerged in materialism," that is, to most of us in a chaotic and disenchanted world. To the unbeliever who has rather smugly despised the churchgoer for seeking an easy consolation, she reveals the secret of his own cowardice, suggesting that his agnosticism may itself be only an opiate, a dodge to avoid facing the terror of God's reality and the awful burden of his love.

She refused to cut herself off from anyone, by refusing to identify herself completely with anyone or any cause. She rejected the temptation to withdraw into a congenial group, once associated with which, she could be disowned by all outside of it. She rather took upon herself the task of sustaining all possible beliefs in their infinite contradictions and on their endless levels of relevance; the smugness of the false elect, the materialism of the shallowly rebellious, self-deceit and hypocrisy, parochialism and atheism—from each she extracted its partial truth, and endured the larger portion of error. She chose to submit to a kind of perpetual invisible crucifixion; her final relationship to all those she would not disown became that of the crucified to the cross.

The French editors of Simone Weil's works, Gustave Thibon, a lay theologian who was also her friend, and Father Perrin, the nearest thing to a confessor she ever had, have both spoken of Simone Weil's refusal to be baptized as a mere stage in her development, a nonessential flaw in her thinking, which, had she only lived longer, would probably have been remedied. M. Thibon and Father Perrin are, of course, Catholics, and speak as they must out of their great love for Mlle Weil, and their understandable conviction that such holiness could not permanently have stayed outside of the Church; but from Simone Weil's own point of view, her outsideness was the very *essence* of her position. This is made especially clear in the present volume.

"I feel," she wrote once, "that it is necessary to me, prescribed for me, to be alone, an outsider and alienated from every human context whatsoever." And on another occasion, she jotted in her journal the self-reminder, "Preserve your solitude!" What motivated her was no selfish desire to withdraw from the ordinary concourse of men, but precisely the opposite impulse. She knew that one remains alienated from a particular allegiance, not by vainly attempting to deny all beliefs, but precisely by sharing them all. To have become rooted in the context of a particular religion, Simone Weil felt, would on the one hand, have exposed her to what she calls "the patriotism of the Church," with a consequent blindness to the faults of her own group and the virtues of others, and would, on the other hand, have separated her from the common condition here below, which finds us all "outsiders, uprooted, in exile." The most terrible of crimes is to collaborate in the uprooting of others in an already alienated world; but the greatest of virtues is to uproot oneself for the sake of one's neighbors and of God. "It is necessary to uproot oneself. Cut down the tree and make a cross and carry it forever after."

Especially at the moment when the majority of mankind is "submerged in materialism," Simone Weil felt she could not detach herself from them by undergoing baptism. To be able to love them as they were, in all their blindness, she would have to know them as they were; and to know them, she would have to go among them disguised in the garments of their own disbelief. In so far as Christianity had become an exclusive sect, it would have to be remade into a "total Incarnation of faith," have to become truly "catholic," catholic enough to include the myths of the dark-skinned peoples from a world untouched by the Churches of the West, as well as the insights of post-Enlightenment liberals, who could see in organized religion only oppression and bitterness and pride.

". . . in our present situation," she wrote, "universality . . . has to be fully explicit." And that explicit universality, she felt, must find a mouthpiece in a new kind of saint, for "today it is not nearly enough merely to be a saint, but we must have the saintliness demanded by the present moment, a new saintliness, itself also without precedent." The new kind of saint must possess a special "genius," capable of blending Christianity and Stoicism, the love of God and "filial piety for the city of the world"; a passive sort of "genius" that would enable him to act as a "neutral medium," like water, "indifferent to all ideas without exception, even atheism and materialism . . ."

Simone Weil felt that she could be only the forerunner and foreteller of such a saint; for her, humility forbade her thinking of herself as one capable of a "new revelation of the universe and human destiny . . . the unveiling of a large portion of truth and beauty hitherto hidden . . ." Yet she is precisely the saint she prophesied!

Despite her modesty, she spoke sometimes as if she were aware that there was manifest in the circumstances of her birth (she had been born into an agnostic family of Jewish descent) a special providence, a clue to a special mission. While it was true, she argued in her letters to Catholic friends, that the earlier Saints had all loved the Church and had been baptized into it, on the other hand, they had all been born and brought up in the Church, as she had *not*. "I should betray the truth," she protested, "that is to say, the aspect of the truth that I see, if I left the point, where I have been since my birth, at the intersection of Christianity and everything that is not Christianity."

It must not be thought that she was even troubled by the question of formally becoming a Christian; it vexed her devout Catholic friends and for *their* sakes she returned again and again to the problem; but, as for herself, she was at peace. Toward the end of her life, the mystic vision came to her almost daily, and she did not have to wonder (in such matters, she liked to say, one does not believe or disbelieve; one *knows* or does not know) if there were salvation outside an organized sect; she was a living witness that the visible Church and the invisible congregation of the saints are never one. "I have never for a second had the feeling that God wanted me in the Church.... I never doubted.... I believe that now it can be concluded that God does not want me in the Church."

It is because she was capable of remaining on the threshold of organized religion, "without moving, quite still ... indefinitely . . ." that Simone Weil speaks to all of us with special authority, an Outsider to outsiders, our kind of saint, whom we have needed (whether we have known it or not) "as a plague-stricken town needs doctors."

To what then does she bear witness? To the uses of exile

9

and suffering, to the glory of annihilation and absurdity, to the unforeseen miracle of love. Her life and work form a single document, a document which we can still not read clearly, though clearly enough, perhaps, for our needs. On the one hand, the story of Simone Weil's life is still guarded by reticence; and on the other hand, her thought comes to us in fragmentary form. She completed no large-scale work; she published in her lifetime no intimate testimony to the secret religious life that made of her last few years a series of experiences perhaps unequaled since St. Theresa and St. John of the Cross. If she has left any detailed account of those experiences we have not yet seen it.

Since her death, four volumes of her work have been published in France. *La Pesanteur et la Grâce* (*Gravity and Grace*), is a selection from her diaries, chosen and topically rearranged by Gustave Thibon; the effect is that of a modern *Pensées*—no whole vision, but a related, loosely linked body of aphorisms, always illuminating and direct, sometimes extraordinarily acute. We do not know, of course, what M. Thibon has chosen to omit; and he has not even told us how large a proportion of the notebooks he has included in his selection.

L'Enracinement (*The Need for Roots*) is the longest single piece left by Simone Weil. Begun at the request of the Free French Government in exile, it takes off from a consideration of the religious and social principles upon which a truly Christian French nation might be built and touches upon such subjects as the humanizing of factory work, the need for freedom of purely speculative thought, and the necessity for expunging from our books a false notion of the heroic which makes us all guilty of the rise of Hitler. It is a fascinating though uneven book, in parts ridiculous, in parts profound, but motivated throughout by the pity and love Simone Weil felt in contemplating a society that had made of the apparatus of government an oppressive machine by separating the secular and religious.

The third book, of which the present volume is a translation, is in many ways the most representative and appealing of the three. It is not, of course, a whole, but a chance collection, entrusted to Father Perrin during the time just before Simone Weil's departure for America. It includes some material, originally written as early as 1937, though recast in the final years of her life; but in the main it represents the typical concerns of the end of Simone Weil's life, after she had reached a haven of certainty. Among the documents (which survived a confiscation by the Gestapo) are six letters, all but one written to Father Perrin, of which letter IV, the "Spiritual Autobiography," is of special importance. Among the essays, the meditation on the *Pater Noster* possesses great interest, for this was the single prayer by which Simone Weil attained almost daily the Divine Vision of God; and the second section of the study called "Forms of the Implicit Love of God," I find the most moving and beautiful piece of writing Simone Weil ever did.

Another volume of her collected essays and meditations, under the title *La Connaissance Surnaturelle* (Supernatural Knowledge) has recently appeared in France, and several other volumes made up of extracts from her notebooks are to be published soon. Simone Weil apparently left behind her a large body of fragments, drafts, and unrevised sketches, which a world that finds in her most casual words insights and illuminations will not be content to leave in manuscript.

Several of her poems and prose pieces, not included in any of these volumes, have been published in various French magazines (notably in *Cahiers de Sud*) and three or four of her political essays have appeared in this country in *Politics*. But the only really consequential study, aside from those in the three books, is her splendid, though absurdly and deliberately partial, interpretation of the *Iliad*, which has been excellently translated into English by Mary McCarthy and published in pamphlet form under the title of *The Iliad: or, the Poem of Force*.

These are the chief sources of her thought; and the introductions to the volumes edited by M. Thibon and Father Perrin provide, along with briefer personal tributes printed at the time of her death, the basic information we have about her life. In a profound sense, her life is her chief work, and without some notion of her biography it is impossible to know her total meaning. On the other hand, her books are extensions of her life; they are not *literature*, not even in the sense that the writings of a theologically oriented author like Kierkegaard are literature. They are confessions and testimonies—sometimes agonized cries or dazzled exclamations—motivated by the desire to say just how it was with her, regardless of all questions of form or beauty of style. They have, however, a charm of directness, an appealing purity of tone that makes it possible to read them (Simone Weil would have hated to acknowledge it!) for the sheer pleasure of watching a subtle mind capture in words the most elusive of paradoxes, or of contemplating an absolute love striving to communicate itself in spite of the clumsiness of language.

HER LIFE

We do not know, as yet, a great deal about the actual facts of Simone Weil's life. Any attempt at biographical reconstruction runs up against the reticence and reserve of her parents, who are still living, and even more critically, it encounters her own desire to be anonymous—to deny precisely those elements in her experience, which to the biographer are most interesting. She was born in 1909, into a family apparently socially secure (her father was a doctor) and "completely agnostic." Though her ancestors had been Jewish, the faith had quite disappeared in her immediate family, and where it flourished still among remoter relatives, it had become something cold, oppressive, and meaninglessly legalistic to a degree that made Simone Weil all of her life incapable of judging fairly the merits of Judaism. She appeared to have no sense of alienation from the general community connected with her Jewishness (though in appearance she seems to have fitted exactly a popular stereotype of the Jewish face), but grew up with a feeling of belonging quite firmly to a world whose values were simply "French," that is to say, a combination of Greek and secularized Christian elements.

Even as a child, she seems to have troubled her parents, to whom being comfortable was an end of life, and who refused to or could not understand her mission. They frustrated again and again, with the greatest of warmth and good will, her attempts to immolate herself for the love of God. Her father and mother came to represent, in an almost archetypal struggle with her, the whole solid bourgeois world, to whom a hair shirt is a scandal, and suffering only a blight to be eliminated by science and proper familial care. Yet she loved her parents as dearly as they loved her, though she was from childhood quite incapable of overt demonstrations of affection.

At the age of five, she refused to eat sugar, as long as the soldiers at the front were not able to get it. The war had brought the sense of human misery into her protected milieu for the first time, and her typical pattern of response was already set: to deny herself what the most unfortunate were unable to enjoy. There is in her reaction, of course, something of the hopeless guilt of one born into a favored position in a society with sharp class distinctions. Throughout her career, there was to be a touch of the absurd in her effort to identify herself utterly with the most exploited groups in society (whose own major desire was to rise up into the class from which she was trying to abdicate), and being continually "rescued" from the suffering she sought by parents and friends. A little later in her childhood, she declared that she would no longer wear socks, while the children of workers had to go without them. This particular gesture, she was later to admit in a typically scrupulous bit of self-analysis, might have been prompted as much by an urge to tease her mother as by an unselfish desire to share the lot of the poor.

At fourteen, she passed through the darkest spiritual crisis of her life, feeling herself pushed to the very verge of suicide by an acute sense of her absolute unworthiness, and by the onslaught of migraine headaches of an unbearable intensity. The headaches never left her afterward, not even in her moments of extremest joy; her very experiences of Divine Love would come to her strained through that omnipresent pain which attacked her, as she liked to say, "at the intersection of body and soul." She came later to think of that torment, intensified by the physical hardships to which she compulsively exposed herself, as a special gift; but in early adolescence, it was to her only a visible and outward sign of her inner misery at her own total lack of talent.

The root of her troubles seems to have been her relationship with her brother, a mathematical prodigy, beside whose brilliance she felt herself stumbling and stupid. Her later academic successes and the almost universal respect accorded her real intelligence seem never to have convinced her that she had any intellectual talent. The chance phrase of a visitor to her mother, overheard when she was quite young, had brought the whole problem to a head. Simone Weil never forgot the words. "One is genius itself," the woman had said, pointing to the boy; and then, indicating Simone, "the other beauty!" It is hard to say whether she was more profoundly disturbed by the imputation of a beauty she did not possess, or by the implicit denial of genius.

Certainly, forever afterward, she did her best to destroy what in her was "beautiful" and superficially charming, to turn herself into the antimask of the appealing young girl. The face in her photographs is absolute in its refusal to be charming, an exaggeration, almost a caricature of the intellectual Jewess. In a sentence or two, Father Perrin recreates her for us in her typical costume: the oversize brown beret, the shapeless cape, the large, floppy shoes, and emerging from this disguise, the clumsy, imperious gestures. We hear, too, the unmusical voice that completes the ensemble, monotonous, almost merciless in its insistence. Only in her writing, is Simone Weil betrayed into charm; in her life, she made a principle of avoiding it. "A beautiful woman," she writes, "looking at her image in the mirror may very well believe the image is herself. An ugly woman knows it is not."

But though her very appearance declares her physical humility, we are likely to be misled about Simone Weil's attitude toward her own intelligence. Father Perrin tells us that he never saw her yield a point in an argument with anybody, but on the other hand, he is aware, as we should be, too, of her immense humbleness in the realm of ideas. Never was she able to believe that she truly possessed the quality she saw so spectacularly in her own brother, the kind of "genius" that was honestly to be envied in so far as it promised not merely "exterior success" but also access to the very "kingdom of truth."

She did not commit suicide, but she passed beyond the temptation without abandoning her abysmal sense of her own stupidity. Instead, she learned painfully the *uses* of stupidity. To look at a mathematical problem one has inexcusably missed, she writes, is to learn the true discipline of humility. In the contemplation of our crimes or our sins, even of our essential proneness to evil, there are temptations to pride, but in the contemplation of the failures of our intelligence, there is only degradation and the sense of shame. To know that one is mediocre is "to be on the true way."

Besides, when one has no flair for geometry (it is interesting that her examples come always from the field of her brother's special competence) the working of a problem becomes not the really irrelevant pursuit of an "answer," but a training in "attention," which is the essence of prayer. And this in turn opens to us the source of a higher kind of genius, which has nothing to do with natural talent and everything to do with Grace. "Only a kind of perversity can force the friends of God to deprive themselves of genius, because it is enough for them to demand it of their Father in the name of Christ, to have a superabundance of genius..." Yet even this final consideration never brought her absolute peace. She wrote toward the end of her life that she could never read the parable of the "barren fig tree" without a shudder, seeing in the figure always a possible portrait of herself, naturally impotent, and yet somehow, in the inscrutable plan of God, cursed for that impotence.

However she may have failed her own absolute standards, she always seems to have pleased her teachers. At the *Ecole Normale Supérieure*, where she studied from 1928 to 1931, finally attaining her *agregée de philosophie* at the age of 22, she was a student of the philosopher Alain, who simply would not believe the report of her early death years afterward. "She will come back surely," he kept repeating. "It isn't true!" It was, perhaps, under his instruction that the love of Plato, so important in her thought, was confirmed in her once and for all.

But at that point of her career she had been influenced by

Marx as well as the Greek philosophers; and it was as an earnest and committed radical, though one who had never joined a particular political party, that she took up her first teaching job at Le Puy. It was a time for radicals—those utterly bleak years at the pit of a world-wide depression. She seems, in a way not untypical of the left-wing intellectual in a small town, to have horrified the good citizens of Le Puy by joining the workers in their sports, marching with them in their picket lines, taking part with the unemployed in their pick and shovel work, and refusing to eat more than the rations of those on relief, distributing her surplus food to the needy. The bourgeois mind seems to have found it as absurd for this awkward girl to be playing ball with workers, as to be half-starving herself because of principles hard to understand. As for crying for a Revolution—!

A superintendent of instruction was called in to threaten Simone Weil with revocation of her teacher's license, at which she declared proudly that she would consider such a revocation "the crown of her career!" There is a note of false bravado in the response, betraying a desire to become a "cause," to attain a spectacular martyrdom. It is a common flaw in the revolutionary activity of the young; but fortunately for Simone Weil, this kind of dénouement, of which she would have been ashamed later, was denied her. She was only a young girl, harmless, and her license was not revoked. Irked at the implied slur, perhaps, and certainly dissatisfied in general with halfway participation in the class struggle of a teacher-sympathizer, she decided to become a worker once and for all, by taking a job at the Renault auto plant.

It is hard to know how to judge the venture. Undoubtedly, there is in it something a little ridiculous: the resolve of the Vassar girl of all lands to "share the experience" of the working class; and the inevitable refusal behind that resolve to face up to the fact that the freedom to *choose* a worker's life, and the consciousness of that choice, which can never be sloughed off, make the dreamed-of total identification impossible. And yet for the sake of that absurd vision, Simone Weil suffered under conditions exacerbated by her sensibility and physical weakness beyond anything the ordinary worker had to bear; the job "entered into her body," and the ennui and misery of working-class life entered into her soul, making of her a "slave," in a sense she could only understand fully later, when her religious illumination had come.

She was always willing to take the step beyond the trivially silly; and the ridiculous pushed far enough, absurdity compounded, becomes something else—the Absurd as a religious category, the madness of the Holy fool beside which the wisdom of this world is revealed as folly. This point Simone Weil came to understand quite clearly. Of the implicit forms of the love of God, she said, ". . . in a sense they are absurd, they are mad," and this she knew to be their special claim. Even unhappiness, she learned, in order to be pure must be a little absurd. The very superiority of Christ over all the martyrs is that he is not anything so solemn as a martyr at all, but a "slave," a criminal among criminals, "only a little more ridiculous. For unhappiness is ridiculous."

An attack of pleurisy finally brought Simone Weil's factory experience to an end (there were always her parents waiting to rescue her), but having rested for a while, just long enough to regain some slight measure of strength, she set off for Spain to support the Loyalists, vowing all the while that she would not ever learn to use the gun they gave her. She talked about Spain with the greatest reluctance in later years, despite the fact, or perhaps because it was undoubtedly for her, as for many in her generation, a critical experience: the efflorescence and the destruction of the revolutionary dream. From within and without the Marxist hope was defeated in a kind of model demonstration, a paradigm for believers. Simone Weil was fond of quoting the Homeric phrase about "justice, that fugitive from the camp of the victors" but in those years it was absent from the camp of victor and vanquished alike. Not even defeat could purify the revolution!

While the struggle in Spain sputtered toward its close, Simone Weil endured a personal catastrophe even more anticlimactic; she was wounded—by accident! The fate that preserved her throughout her life for the antiheroic heroism of her actual death, brought this episode, too, to a bathetic conclusion. Concerned with the possibilities of combining participation and nonviolence, pondering the eternal, she forgot the "real" world of missteps and boiling oil, and ineptly burned herself, a victim of that clumsiness which seems to have been an essential aspect of her denial of the physical self. Badly hurt and poorly cared for, she was rescued from a field hospital by her parents—once more coming between her and her desired agony!

The Spanish adventure was her last purely political gesture; afterward, during the Second World War, she was to work up some utterly impractical plan for being parachuted into France to carry spiritual solace to the fighters in the underground resistance; and she was even to consider at one point going to the Soviet Union, where she could doubtless not have lived in freedom for a month. Among the Communists in France she had been known as a Trotskyite, and had once been threatened with physical violence for delivering an anti-Stalinist report at a trade union convention. But at a moment when the Russians were retreating before the German attack, she felt obliged to "add a counterweight," in order to restore that equilibrium which could alone make life here below bearable. One can barely imagine her in the field with the Red Army, this quixotic, suffering "friend of God," flanked by the self-assured killers of "Fascist Beasts," and carrying in her hand the gun that would doubtless have blown off her fingers had she tried to fire it.

These later projects were, as their very "impossibility" attests, different in kind from her early practical ventures: the picketing with the unemployed, the participation in Spain. She had passed into the realm of the politics of the absurd, of metapolitics, having decided that "the revolution is the opiate of the people," and that the social considered in itself is "a trap of traps ... an *ersatz* divinity ... irremediably the domain of the devil." The lure of the social she believed to be her special temptation. Against the love of self she was armored by her very temperament. "No one loves himself," she wrote in her journal. "Man wants to be an egoist and cannot." But a nostalgia for collective action seemed ever on the point of overwhelming her defenses. Simply to join together with others in any group whatsoever would have been for her "delicious." "I know that if at this moment I had before me a group of twenty young Germans singing Nazi songs in chorus," she once said, "a part of my soul would instantly become Nazi. . . ." Yet, the "we" can lead away from God, she knew, as dangerously as the "I." "It is wrong to be an 'I,' but it is worse to be a 'we,'" she warned herself. "The city gives us the feeling of being at home. Cultivate the feeling of being at home in exile."

Yet charity took her continually back into the world of social action. "Misery must be eliminated in so far as possible from life in society, for misery is useful only in respect to grace, and society is not a society of the elect. There will always be enough misery for the elect." If there is a certain inconsistency in her position, it is easy to forgive. Even the "wrong" politics of her revolutionary youth she would not write off as wholly mistaken; she never repented her early radicalism, understanding it as a providential discipline, through which she had been unconsciously learning how to emancipate her imagination from its embroilment with the social. "Meditation on the social mechanism is a purification of the first importance in this regard. To contemplate the social is as good a means of purification as retiring from the world. That is why I was not wrong in staying with politics for so long."

It was after her Spanish experience that Simone Weil

reached the critical point of conversion; but the decisive event in her spiritual education had been, she always felt, her work in the factory. She had not known what she was seeking at the machine, but she had found it nonetheless: branded with the red mark of the slave, she had become incapable of resisting "the religion of slaves." In one sense, Simone Weil insisted afterward, she had not needed to be converted; she had always been *implicitly*, in "secret" even from her lower self, a Christian; but she had never knelt, she had never prayed, she had never entered a Church, she had never even posed to herself the question of God's existence. "I may say that never in my life have I 'sought for God,'" she said toward the end of her life; but she had been all the time waiting, without daring to define what she awaited.

Taken off by her parents to Portugal to recuperate from her burns and her chagrin, she made her way to Solesmes, where, listening to a Gregorian chant at the moment when her migraine was at its worst, she experienced the joy and bitterness of Christ's passion as a real event, though still so abstractly that she did not attach to it any name. And there, too, she had met a young English Catholic, who introduced her to the work of the British metaphysical poets of the seventeenth century, and so gave her a key to the beyond, in the place of conventional prayer to which she had not yet been able to turn.

Like no saint before her, Simone Weil distrusted the conventional apparatus of piety and grace; and it is typical of her role that it was through forms of art acceptable to the most skeptical anti-Christian (Gregorian chant and meta-physical poetry—two of the special rediscoveries of our irreligious time) that she approached her encounter with God. "In a moment of intense physical suffering," she tells us, "when I was forcing myself to feel love, but without desiring to give a name to that love, I felt, without being in any way prepared for it (for I had never read the mystical writers) a presence more personal, more certain, more real than that of a human being, though inaccessible to the senses and the imagination. . . ." She had been repeating to herself a piece by George Herbert, when the presence came. "I used to think I was merely reciting it as a beautiful poem," she writes, "but without my knowing it the recitation had the virtue of a prayer." It is worth quoting the poem as a whole, for its imagery is vital, as we shall see later, to an understanding of Simone Weil's essential thought.

> Love bade me welcome: yet my soul drew back,
>   Guiltie of lust and sinne.
> But quick-ey'd Love, observing me grow slack
>   From my first entrance in,
> Drew nearer to me, sweetly questioning,
>   If I lack'd any thing.
>
> A guest, I answer'd, worthy to be here:
>   Love said, You shall be he.
> I the unkinde, ungratefull? Ah my deare,
>   I cannot look on thee.
> Love took my hand, and smiling did reply,
>   Who made the eyes but I?

Truth Lord, but I have marr'd them: let my shame
   Go where it doth deserve.
And know you not, sayes Love, who bore the blame?
   My deare, then I will serve.
You must sit down, sayes Love, and taste my meat:
   So I did sit and eat.

Even after such an experience, this astonishingly stubborn friend of God could not *for more than five years* bring herself conventionally to pray (though she tells us that in 1937 she knelt for the first time, at the shrine in Assisi), finally persuading herself to say the *Pater Noster* daily with so special a concentration that apparently at each repetition, Christ himself "descended and took her." It is her remarkable freedom from, her actual shamefastness before the normal procedures of Christian worship that lend a special authority to Simone Weil's testimony. Nothing comes to her as a convention or a platitude; it is as if she is driven to reinvent everything from the beginning. Of her first mystical experience she writes, "God had mercifully prevented me from reading the mystics, so that it would be clear to me that I had not fabricated an absolutely unexpected encounter." Surely, no mystic has ever been so scrupulously his own skeptical examiner.

Afterward, Simone Weil found in St. John of the Cross and the *Bhagavad-Gita* accounts of encounters similar to her own; and she even decided upon rereading her old master Plato in the light of her new experience that he, too, must have achieved the mystical union. Before her own encounter, she had thought that all such alleged experiences could be only a turning of the natural orientation of the sexual desire toward an imaginary object labeled God—a degrading self-indulgence, "lower than a debauch." To distinguish her own secret life from such *ersatz* mysticism became one of the main objects of her thought.

After her first mystical union, the inner existence of Simone Weil becomes much more important than anything that superficially happens to her. Even the War itself, the grossest fact of our recent history, shrinks in the new perspective. Nonetheless, Simone Weil continued to immerse herself in the misery of daily life. Driven by her constant desire not to separate herself from the misfortune of others, she refused to leave Paris until it was declared an open city, after which she moved with her parents to Marseilles. But there she was caught by the anti-Jewish laws of the Vichy Government which made it impossible for her to teach any longer; and so she went to Gustave Thibon, a lay theologian, in charge of a Catholic agricultural colony in the South of France. Under his guidance, she worked in the vineyards with the peasants (whom she astonished and bored with lectures on the Upanishads!), sleeping as they slept, and eating their meager fare until her feeble health broke down once more. M. Thibon at first immensely mistrusted her motives—a radical intellectual "returning to the soil!"—then became closely attached to her, and it was to him that she entrusted her journals and occasional jottings, which he finally decided to publish after her death despite her request to the contrary.

The chief external influence on Simone Weil during these last years of her spiritual progress was not M. Thibon, but

Father Perrin, with whom she was apparently able to talk as she had never been able to before, and to whom she communicated what of her secrets could be spoken at all. He was truly and deeply her friend. One has the sense of Simone Weil as a woman to whom "sexual purity" is as instinctive as breath; to whom, indeed, any kind of sentimental life is scarcely necessary. But a few lines in one of her absolutely frank and unguarded letters to Father Perrin reveal a terrible loneliness which only he was able to mitigate, to some degree, and a vulnerability which only he knew how to spare. "I believe that, except for you, all human beings to whom I have ever given, through my friendship, the power to harm easily, have sometimes amused themselves by doing so, frequently or rarely, consciously or unconsciously, but all of them at one time or another. . . ."

It is no evil in them, she hastens to add, that prompts this infliction of pain, but an instinct, almost mechanical, like that which makes the other animals in the chicken yard fall on the wounded hen. The figure of the wounded hen is one to which she returns elsewhere, and in contemplating it, one knows suddenly the immense sensitivity beneath the inflexible surface, her terrible need *not* to be laughed at or pitied for her patent absurdities. One remembers another heart-rending figure she used once to describe herself, "Indeed for other people, in a sense I do not exist. I am the color of dead leaves, like certain unnoticed insects." And the phrases from her journal recur, "never seek friendship . . . never permit oneself to dream of friendship . . . friendship is a miracle!"

It was with Father Perrin that Simone Weil argued out the question of baptism: Would she lose her intellectual freedom in entering the Church? Did Catholicism have in it too much of those "great beasts" Israel and Rome? Did Christianity deny the beauty of this world? Did excommunication make of the Church an instrument of exclusion? Her friendship for the priest made her problem especially difficult: she did not want to hurt him personally by refusing baptism at his hands, nor did she certainly want to accept merely out of her love for him.

In the end, she decided to wait for an express command from God, "except perhaps at the moment of death." Searching, she believed, leads only to error; obedience is the sole way to truth. "If," she wrote in one of her most splendid paradoxes, "it were conceivable that one might be damned by obeying God and saved by disobeying him; I would nonetheless obey him." The role of the future spouse is to wait; and it is to this "waiting for God" that the title of the present collection refers. Simone Weil finally remained on the threshold of the Church, crouching there for the love of all of us who are not inside, all the heretics, the secular dreamers, the prophesiers in strange tongues; "without budging," she wrote, "immobile, ἐν ὑπομένῃ ... only now my heart has been transported, forever I hope, into the Holy Sacrament revealed on the altar."

In May, 1942, she finally agreed to accompany her parents, who had been urging her for a long time, and set sail for America. Before her departure she remarked ruefully to a friend, "Don't you think the sea might serve me as a baptismal font?" But America proved intolerable to her; simply to *be* in so secure a land was, no matter how one tried to live, to enjoy what most men could not attain. She finally returned to England, where she tried desperately to work out some scheme for re-entering France, and where she refused to eat any more than the rations allowed her countrymen in the occupied territory. Exhausted and weakened by her long fast, she permitted herself to be borne off into the country by well-meaning protectors, but on August 24th in 1943, she succeeded at last in dying, completing the process of "de-creation" at which she had aimed all her life.

HER METHOD

Simone Weil's writing as a whole is marked by three characteristic devices: extreme statement or paradox; the equilibrium of contradictions; and exposition by myth. As the life of Simone Weil reflects a desire to insist on the absolute even at the risk of being absurd, so her writing tends always toward the extreme statement, the formulation that shocks by its willingness to push to its ultimate conclusion the kind of statement we ordinarily accept with the tacit understanding that no one will take it *too* seriously. The outrageous (from the natural point of view) ethics of Christianity, the paradoxes on which it is based are a scandal to common sense; but we have protected ourselves against them by turning them imperceptibly into platitudes. It is Simone Weil's method to revivify them, by recreating them in all their pristine offensiveness.

"He who gives bread to the famished sufferer for the love of God will not be thanked by Christ. He has already had his reward in this thought itself. Christ thanks those who do not know to whom they are giving food." Or "Ineluctable necessity, misery, distress, the crushing weight of poverty and of work that drains the spirit, cruelty, torture, violent death, constraint, terror, sickness—all these are God's love!" Or "Evil is the beautiful obedience of matter to the will of God."

Sometimes the primary function of her paradoxes is to remind us that we live in a world where the eternal values are reversed; it is as if Simone Weil were bent on proving to us, by our own uncontrollable drawing back from what we most eagerly should accept, that we do not truly believe those things to which we declare allegiance. ". . . every time I think of the crucifixion of Christ I commit the sin of envy." "Suffering: superiority of man over God. We needed the Incarnation to keep that superiority from becoming a scandal!"

Or sometimes it is our sentimentality that is being attacked, that *ersatz* of true charity which is in fact its worst enemy, "[Christ] did not however prescribe the abolition of penal justice. He allowed stoning to continue. Wherever it is done with justice, it is therefore he who throws the first stone." "Bread and stone are love. We must eat the bread and lay ourselves open to the stone, so that it may sink as deeply as possible into our flesh."

Or the paradox may have as its point merely the proving of the *impossibility* of God's justice, the inconsequentiality of virtue and grace. "A Gregorian chant bears testimony as effectively as the death of a martyr." "... a Latin prose or a geometry problem, even though they are done wrong, may be of great service one day, provided we devote the right kind of effort to them. Should the occasion arise, they can one day make us better able to give someone in affliction exactly the help required to save him, at the supreme moment of his need."

Corresponding to Simone Weil's basic conviction that no widely held belief is utterly devoid of truth is a dialectical method in which she balances against each other contrary propositions, not in order to arrive at a synthesis in terms of a "golden mean," but rather to achieve an equilibrium of truths. "One must accept all opinions," she has written, "but then arrange them in a vertical order, placing them at appropriate levels." Best of all exercises for the finding of truth is the confrontation of statements that seem absolutely to contradict each other. "Method of investigation—" Simone Weil once jotted down in a note to herself, "as soon as one has arrived at any position, try to find in what sense the contrary is true."

When she is most faithful to this method, her thought is most satisfactory; only where some overwhelming prejudice prevents her from honoring contradictions is she narrow and unilluminating—as for instance, toward Israel, Rome, Aristotle, or Corneille. These unwitting biases must be distinguished from her deliberate strategic emphases, her desire to "throw the counterweight" on the side of a proposition against which popular judgment is almost solidly arrayed; as she does most spectacularly by insisting, in the teeth of our worship of happiness and success, that "unhappiness" is the essential road to God, and the supreme evidence of God's love.

One can see her method of equilibrium most purely in her remarks on immortality of the soul, in her consideration of the rival Protestant and Catholic theories of the Eucharist, and especially in her approach to the existence of God. "A case of contradictories, both of them true. There is a God. There is no God. Where is the problem? I am quite sure that there is a God in the sense that I am sure my love is no illusion. I am quite sure there is no God, in the sense that I am sure there is nothing which resembles what I can conceive when I say that word...."

There are three main factors that converge in Simone Weil's interest in the myth (this is yet another aspect of her thought with which the contemporary reader of Jung and Joyce and Eliot and Mann feels particularly at home): first, there is the example of her master, Plato, who at all the great crises of his thought falls back on the mythic in search of a subtle and total explication; second, there is her own belief in multiple revelation, her conviction that the archetypal poetries of people everywhere restate the same truths in different metaphoric languages; and third, there is her sense of myth as the special gospel of the poor, a treasury of insights into the Beauty of the World, which Providence has bestowed on poverty alone, but which, in our uprooted world, the alienated oppressed can no longer decipher for themselves.

To redeem the truths of the myths, they must be "translated." Sometimes this is a relatively simple process of substituting for unfamiliar names, ones that belong to our own system of belief: Zeus is God the Father, Bacchus God the Son; Dionysus and Osiris "are (in a certain manner) Christ himself." In the fragment of Sophocles, Electra is the human soul and Orestes is Christ; but in this latter example we are led, once we have identified the protagonists, to a complex religious truth: as Electra loves the absence of Orestes more than the presence of any other, so must we love God, who is by definition "absent" from the material world, more than the "real," present objects that surround us.

In a similar manner, other folk stories and traditional poems can lead toward revelations of fundamental truths: the "two winged companions" of an Upanishad, who sit on a single branch, one eating the fruit of the tree, the other looking at it, represent the two portions of the soul: the one that would contemplate the good, the other (like Eve in the Garden) that would consume it. Or the little tailor in Grimm's fairy tale who beats a giant in a throwing contest by hurling into the air a bird rather than a stone teaches us something about the nature of Grace. And finally, we discover from "all the great images of folklore and mythology" what Simone Weil considers to be the truth most necessary to our salvation, namely, "it is God who seeks man."

The fate of the world, she knew, is decided out of time; and it is in myth that mankind has recorded its sense of its true history, the eternal "immobile drama" of necessity and evil, salvation and grace.

33

HER ESSENTIAL THOUGHT

It is no accident that Simone Weil has left behind no single summation of her thought; for she is not in any sense a systematic thinker. Some of her profoundest insights were flashed off as detached aphorisms; and, as we have seen, she sought, rather than avoided, inconsistency. To reduce her ideas to a unified body of dogma would be, therefore, misleading and unfair; yet there are certain central concepts to which she always returned, key images that she might extend or vary, but which she could never entirely escape. These figures which adumbrate the core of her commitment are those of eating, looking, and walking toward; of gravity (*pesanteur*) and light; of slavery, nudity, poverty, and decreation.

The first group seems almost instinctive, rooted below the level of thought in Simone Weil's temperament itself, and provides a way into the others. The whole pattern of her life is dominated by the concepts of eating and not eating; from her childhood refusal of sugar, through her insistence at Le Puy on eating only as much as the relief allowance of the unemployed, to her death from semistarvation in England, her virtue seems naturally to have found its expression in attitudes toward food. The very myths that most attracted her: the Minotaur, Eve and the apple, the two birds of the Upanishad are based on metaphors of eating; and the final line of the poem of George Herbert, which was the occasion of her first mystical experience, reads, we remember, "So I did sit and eat."

There are two kinds of "eating" for Simone Weil, the "eating" of beauty and the beloved here below, which is a grievous error, "what one eats is destroyed, it is no longer real," and the miraculous "eating" in Heaven, where one consumes and is consumed by his God. "The great trouble in human life is that looking and eating are two different operations. Only beyond the sky, in the country inhabited by God, are they one and the same single operation. . . . It may be that vice, depravity, and crime are nearly always, or even perhaps always, in their essence, attempts to eat beauty, to eat what we should only look at."

Here below we must be content to be eternally hungry; indeed, we must *welcome* hunger, for it is the sole proof we have of the reality of God, who is the only sustenance that can satisfy us, but one which is "absent" in the created world. "The danger is not lest the soul should doubt whether there is any bread [God], but lest, by a lie, it should persuade itself that it is not hungry. It can only persuade itself of this by lying, for the reality of its hunger is not a belief, it is a certainty."

Not to deny one's hunger and still not to eat what is forbidden, there is the miracle of salvation! It is true even on the level of human friendship, "a miracle by which a person consents to view from a certain distance, and without coming any nearer, the very being who is necessary to him as food." And how much more true on the level of the divine! "If [Eve] had been hungry at the moment when she looked at the fruit, if in spite of that she had remained looking at it indefinitely without taking one step toward it, she would have performed a miracle analogous to that of perfect friendship."

It is "looking" which saves and not "eating." "It should also be publicly and officially recognized that religion is nothing else but a looking." Looking, the mere turning of the head toward God, is equated by Simone Weil with desire and that passive effort of "waiting for God" which gives the present book its name; while eating is equated with the will, and the false muscular effort to seize that which can only be freely given. Man's "free will" consists in nothing but the ability to turn, or to refuse to turn, his eyes toward what God holds up before him. "One of the principal truths of Christianity, a truth that goes almost unrecognized today, is that looking is what saves us. The bronze serpent was lifted up so that those who lay maimed in the depths of degradation should be saved by looking upon it."

Besides the temptation to consume what should only be regarded, man is beset by the longing to march toward the inapproachable, which he should be willing merely to look at from afar; and worst of all, he ends by persuading himself that he *has* approached it. "The great error of the Marxists and of all the nineteenth century was to believe that by walking straight ahead one had mounted into the air." What we really want is above us, not ahead of us, and "We cannot take a single step toward heaven. It is not in our power to travel in a vertical direction. If however we look heavenward for a long time, God comes and takes us up." We are free only to change the direction of our glance; we cannot walk into heaven; we cannot rise without being lifted by grace.

The vertical is forbidden to us because the world is the province of gravity and dead weight (*pesanteur*). The whole universe, as we know it through the senses and the imagination, has been turned over by God to the control of brute mechanism, to necessity and blind force, and that primary physical law by which all things eternally *fall*. The very act of creation entailed the withdrawal of the Creator from the created, so that the sum total of God and his world and all of its creatures is, of course, less than God himself. Having withdrawn from the universe so that it might exist, God is powerless within it, ineffective except as his grace penetrates on special occasions, like a ray of light, the dark mechanical realm of unlimited misery.

Yet we must *love* this world, this absence of God by virtue of which we are, for only through it, like the smile of the beloved through pain, can we sense the perfectly nonpresent Being who alone can redeem it. "In the beauty of the world, brute necessity becomes an object of love. What is more beautiful than the action of gravity on the fugitive folds of the sea waves or on the almost eternal folds of the mountains?"

This world is the only reality available to us, and if we do not love it in all its terror, we are sure to end up loving the "imaginary," our own dreams and self-deceits, the utopias of the politicians, or the futile promises of future reward and consolation which the misled blasphemously call "religion." The soul has a million dodges for protecting itself against the acceptance and love of the emptiness, that "maximum distance between God and God," which is the universe; for the price of such acceptance and love is

abysmal misery. And yet it is the only way. "If still persevering in our love, we fall to the point where the soul
cannot keep back the cry 'My God, my God, why hast
thou forsaken me?' if we remain at this point without ceasing to love, we end by touching something that is not affliction, not joy, something that is the central essence,
necessary and pure, something not of the senses, common
to joy and sorrow: the very love of God."

The final crown of the life of holiness is the moment of
utter despair in which one becomes totally a "slave," naked
and abandoned and nailed to the cross in imitation of the
absolute spiritual poverty of Christ. "Extreme affliction ...
is a nail whose point is applied at the very center of the
soul, whose head is all necessity spreading throughout space
and time. . . . He whose soul remains ever turned toward
God though pierced with a nail finds himself nailed to the
center of the universe ... at the intersection of creation
and its Creator ... at the intersection of the arms of the
Cross."

On the cross, deceit is no longer possible; we are forced
to "recognize as real what we would not even have believed
possible," and having yielded ourselves in love to spiritual
poverty, spiritual nudity, to death itself, even to the point
of provisionally renouncing the hope of immortality, we are
ready for the final gesture of obedience: the surrender of
the last vestiges of selfhood. In the ultimate "nuptial yes,"
we must de-create our egos, offer up everything we have
ever meant by "I," so that the Divine Love may pass un-
impeded through the space we once occupied, close again

on Itself. "We are created for this consent, and for this alone."

LESLIE A. FIEDLER

Montana State University
Missoula, Montana
April 29, 1951

LETTERS

LETTER I

Hesitations Concerning Baptism

January 19, 1942

MY DEAR FATHER,

I have made up my mind to write to you ... to bring our conversations about my case to a conclusion—that is to say, pending further developments. I am tired of talking to you about myself, for it is a wretched subject, but I am obliged to do so by the interest you take in me as a result of your charity.

I have been wondering lately about the will of God, what it means, and how we can reach the point of conforming ourselves to it completely—I will tell you what I think about this.

We have to distinguish among three domains. First, that which is absolutely independent of us; it includes all the accomplished facts in the whole universe at the moment and everything that is happening or going to happen later beyond our reach. In this domain everything that comes about is in accordance with the will of God, without any exception. Here then we must love absolutely everything, as a

43

whole and in each detail, including evil in all its forms; notably our own past sins, in so far as they are past (for we must hate them in so far as their root is still present), our own sufferings, past, present, and to come, and—what is by far the most difficult—the sufferings of other men in so far as we are not called upon to relieve them. In other words, we must feel the reality and presence of God through all external things, without exception, as clearly as our hand feels the substance of paper through the penholder and the nib.

The second domain is that which is placed under the rule of the will. It includes the things that are purely natural, close, easily recognized by the intelligence and the imagination, and among which we can make our choice, arranging them from outside so as to provide means to fixed and finite ends. In this domain we have to carry out, without faltering or delay, everything that appears clearly to be a duty. When any duty does not appear clearly, we have sometimes to observe more or less arbitrarily established rules; and sometimes to follow our inclination, but in a limited degree; for one of the most dangerous forms of sin, or perhaps the most dangerous, consists of introducing what is unlimited into a domain that is essentially finite.

The third domain is that of the things, which, without being under the empire of the will, without being related to natural duties, are yet not entirely independent of us. In this domain we experience the compulsion of God's pressure, on condition that we deserve to experience it and exactly to the extent that we deserve to do so. God rewards the soul that thinks of him with attention and love, and he rewards it by exercising a compulsion upon it strictly and mathematically proportionate to this attention and this love. We have to abandon ourselves to the pressure, to run to the exact spot whither it impels us and not go one step farther, even in the direction of what is good. At the same time we must go on thinking about God with ever increasing love and attentiveness, in this way gaining the favor of being impelled ever further and becoming the object of a pressure that possesses itself of an ever-growing proportion of the whole soul. When the pressure has taken possession of the whole soul, we have attained the state of perfection. But whatever stage we may have reached, we must do nothing more than we are irresistibly impelled to do, not even in the way of goodness.

I have also been thinking about the nature of the sacraments, and I will tell you what I think about this subject as well.

The sacraments have a specific value, which constitutes a mystery in so far as they involve a certain kind of contact with God, a contact mysterious but real. At the same time they have a purely human value in so far as they are symbols or ceremonies. Under this second aspect they do not differ essentially from the songs, gestures, and words of command of certain political parties; at least in themselves they are not essentially different; of course they are infinitely different in the doctrine underlying them. I think that most believers, including some who are really persuaded of the opposite, approach the sacraments only as symbols and ceremonies. Foolish as the theory of Durkheim may be in confusing what is religious with what is social, it yet

45

contains an element of truth; that is to say, that the social feeling is so much like the religious as to be mistaken for it. It is like it just as a false diamond is like a real one, so that those who have no spiritual discernment are effectively taken in. For the matter of that, a social and human participation in the symbols and ceremonies of the sacraments is an excellent and healthy thing in that it marks a stage of the journey for those who travel that way. Yet this is not a participation in the sacraments as such. I think that only those who are above a certain level of spirituality can participate in the sacraments as such. For as long as those who are below this level have not reached it, whatever they may do, they cannot be strictly said to belong to the Church.

As far as I am concerned, I think I am below this level. That is why I said to you the other day that I consider myself to be unworthy of the sacraments. This idea does not come, as you imagined, from scrupulosity. It is due, on the one hand, to a consciousness of very definite faults in the order of action and human relations, serious and even shameful faults as you would certainly agree, and moreover fairly frequent. On the other hand, and still more strongly, it is founded on a general sense of inadequacy. I am not saying this out of humility, for if I possessed the virtue of humility, the most beautiful of all the virtues perhaps, I should not be in this miserable state of inadequacy.

To finish with what has to do with me, I say this. The kind of inhibition that keeps me outside the Church is due either to my state of imperfection, or to the fact that my vocation and God's will are opposed to it. In the first case, I cannot get rid of my inhibition by direct means but only indirectly, by becoming less imperfect, if I am helped by grace. To bring this about it is only necessary, on the one hand to avoid faults in the domain of natural things, and on the other, to put ever more attention and love into my thought of God. If it is God's will that I should enter the Church, he will impose this will upon me at the exact moment when I shall have come to deserve that he should so impose it.

In the second case, if it is not his will that I should enter the Church, how could I enter it? I know quite well what you have often repeated to me, that is to say, that baptism is the common way of salvation—at least in Christian countries —and that there is absolutely no reason why I should have an exceptional one of my own. That is obvious. And yet supposing that in fact it should not be given me to take that step, what could I do? If it were conceivable that in obeying God one should bring about one's own damnation while in disobeying him one could be saved, I should still choose the way of obedience.

It seems to me that the will of God is that I should not enter the Church at present. The reason for this I have told you already and it is still true. It is because the inhibition that holds me back is no less strongly to be felt in the moments of attention, love, and prayer than at other times. And yet I was filled with a very great joy when you said the thoughts I confided to you were not incompatible with allegiance to the Church, and that, in consequence, I was not outside it in spirit.

I cannot help still wondering whether in these days when so large a proportion of humanity is submerged in materialism, God does not want there to be some men and women who have given themselves to him and to Christ and who yet remain outside the Church.

In any case, when I think of the act by which I should enter the Church as something concrete, which might happen quite soon, nothing gives me more pain than the idea of separating myself from the immense and unfortunate multitude of unbelievers. I have the essential need, and I think I can say the vocation, to move among men of every class and complexion, mixing with them and sharing their life and outlook, so far that is to say as conscience allows, merging into the crowd and disappearing among them, so that they show themselves as they are, putting off all disguises with me. It is because I long to know them so as to love them just as they are. For if I do not love them as they are, it will not be they whom I love, and my love will be unreal. I do not speak of helping them, because as far as that goes I am unfortunately quite incapable of doing anything as yet. I do not think that in any case I should ever enter a religious order, because that would separate me from ordinary people by a habit. There are some human beings for whom such a separation has no serious disadvantages, because they are already separated from ordinary folk by their natural purity of soul. As for me, on the contrary, as I think I told you, I have the germ of all possible crimes, or nearly all, within me. I became aware of this in the course of a journey, in circumstances I have described to you. The crimes horrified me, but they did not surprise me; I felt the possibility of them within myself; it was actually because I felt this possibility in myself that they filled me with such horror. This natural disposition is dangerous and very painful, but like every variety of natural disposition, it can be put to good purpose if one knows how to make the right use of it with the help of grace. It is the sign of a vocation, the vocation to remain in a sense anonymous, ever ready to be mixed into the paste of common humanity. Now at the present time, the state of men's minds is such that there is a more clearly marked barrier, a wider gulf between a practicing Catholic and an unbeliever than between a religious and a layman.

I know quite well that Christ said: "Whoever shall deny [*i. e.*, disown] me before men, him will I also deny before my Father which is in Heaven." * But disowning Christ does not perhaps mean for everyone and in all cases not belonging to the Church. For some it may only mean not carrying out Christ's precepts, not shedding abroad his spirit, not honoring his name when occasion arises, not being ready to die out of loyalty to him.

I owe you the truth, at the risk of shocking you, and it gives me the greatest pain to shock you. I love God, Christ, and the Catholic faith as much as it is possible for so miserably inadequate a creature to love them. I love the saints through their writings and what is told of their lives—apart from some whom it is impossible for me to love fully or to consider as saints. I love the six or seven Catholics of genuine spirituality whom chance has led me to meet in the course of my life. I love the Catholic liturgy, hymns, architecture,

* St. Matt. 10:33. Simone Weil evidently used a Greek edition of the New Testament and made her own translations of the quoted texts. It was the decision of the publishers and not of the translator in most cases to use the Authorized Version in the English edition of Simone Weil's works.

rites, and ceremonies. But I have not the slightest love for the Church in the strict sense of the word, apart from its relation to all these things that I do love. I am capable of sympathizing with those who have this love, but I do not feel it. I am well aware that all the saints felt it. But then they were nearly all born and brought up in the Church. Anyhow, one cannot make oneself love. All that I can say is that if such a love constitutes a condition of spiritual progress, which I am unaware of, or if it is part of my vocation, I desire that it may one day be granted to me.

It may well be that some of the thoughts I have just confided to you are illusory and defective. In a sense this matters little to me; I do not want to go on examining any more, for at the end of all these reflections I have reached a conclusion which is the pure and simple resolution to stop thinking about the question of my eventual entry into the Church.

It is very possible that after having passed weeks, months, or years without thinking about it all, one day I shall suddenly feel an irresistible impulse to ask immediately for baptism and I shall run to ask for it. For the action of grace in our hearts is secret and silent.

It may also be that my life will come to an end before I have ever felt this impulse. But one thing is absolutely certain. It is that if one day it comes about that I love God enough to deserve the grace of baptism, I shall receive this grace on that very day, infallibly, in the form God wills, either by means of baptism in the strict sense of the word or in some other manner. In that case why should I have any anxiety? It is not my business to think about myself. My business is to think about God. It is for God to think about me.

This is a very long letter. Once again I shall have taken up much more of your time than I ought. I beg you to forgive me. My excuse is that by writing this I have reached a conclusion, for the time being at any rate.

Do believe how truly grateful I am.

SIMONE WEIL

LETTER II

Same Subject

My dear Father,

This is a postscript to the letter that I told you was provisionally a conclusion. I hope for your sake that it will be the only one. I am very much afraid of boring you. But if I do you must blame yourself. It is not my fault if I believe I owe it to you to keep you informed of what I am thinking.

The obstacles of an intellectual order, which until lately stopped me on the threshold of the Church, might if necessary be considered as eliminated, since you do not refuse to accept me just as I am. Yet there are still obstacles.

After thoroughly considering everything, I think this is what they come to. What frightens me is the Church as a social structure. Not only on account of its blemishes, but from the very fact that it is something social. It is not that I am of a very individualistic temperament. I am afraid for the opposite reason. I am aware of very strong gregarious tendencies in myself. My natural disposition is to be very easily influenced, too much influenced, and above all by anything collective. I know that if at this moment I had before me a group of twenty young Germans singing Nazi songs in chorus, a part of my soul would instantly become Nazi. That is a very great weakness, but that is how I am. I think that it is useless to fight directly against natural weaknesses. One has to force oneself to act as though one did not have them in circumstances where a duty makes it imperative; and in the ordinary course of life one has to know these weaknesses, prudently take them into account, and strive to turn them to good purpose; for they are all capable of being put to some good purpose.

I am afraid of the Church patriotism existing in Catholic circles. By patriotism I mean the feeling one has for a terrestrial country. I am afraid of it because I fear to catch it. It is not that the Church appears to me to be unworthy of inspiring such a feeling. It is because I do not want any feeling of such a kind in myself. The word want is not accurate. I *know*, I feel quite certain, that any feeling of this kind, whatever its object, would be fatal for me.

There were some saints who approved of the Crusades or the Inquisition. I cannot help thinking that they were in the wrong. I cannot go against the light of conscience. If I think that on this point I see more clearly than they did, I who am so far below them, I must admit that in this matter they were blinded by something very powerful. This something was the Church seen as a social structure. If this social structure did them harm, what harm would it not do me, who am particularly susceptible to social influences and who am almost infinitely more feeble than they were?

Nothing ever said or written goes so far as the devil's

words to Christ in Saint Luke concerning the kingdoms of the world. "All this power will I give thee and the glory of it, for that is delivered unto me and to whomsoever I will I give it." It follows from this that the social is irremediably the domain of the devil. The flesh impels us to say *me* and the devil impels us to say *us*; or else to say like the dictators *I* with a collective signification. And, in conformity with his particular mission, the devil manufactures a false imitation of what is divine, an *ersatz* divinity.

By social I do not mean everything connected with citizenship, but only collective emotions.

I am well aware that the Church must inevitably be a social structure; otherwise it would not exist. But in so far as it is a social structure, it belongs to the Prince of this World. It is because it is an organ for the preservation and transmission of truth that there is an extreme danger for those who, like me, are excessively open to social influences. For in this way what is purest and what is most defiling look very much the same, and confused under the same words, make an almost undecomposable mixture.

There is a Catholic circle ready to give an eager welcome to whoever enters it. Well, I do not want to be adopted into a circle, to live among people who say "we" and to be part of an "us," to find I am "at home" in any human *milieu* whatever it may be. In saying I do not want this, I am expressing myself badly, for I should like it very much; I should find it all delightful. But I feel that it is not permissible for me. I feel that it is necessary and ordained that I should be alone, a stranger and an exile in relation to every human circle without exception.

This may seem to contradict what I wrote to you about my need to be merged into any human circle in which I moved. To be lost to view in it is not to form part of it, and my capacity to mix with all of them implies that I belong to none.

I do not know if I have succeeded in making you understand these almost inexpressible things.

Such considerations have to do with this world and seem miserably poor when one turns to the supernatural character of the sacraments. But it is precisely the impure mixture in me of supernatural and evil that I fear.

The relation of hunger to food is far less complete, to be sure, but just as real as is that of the act of eating.

It is perhaps not inconceivable that in a being with certain natural propensities, a particular temperament, a given past, a certain vocation, and so on, the desire for and deprivation of the sacraments might constitute a contact more pure than actual participation.

I do not in the least know whether it is like that with me or not. I am well aware that it would be something exceptional, and it seems as though there were always a crazy presumption in claiming that one might be an exception. But the exceptional character may very well be due not to superiority but to inferiority in comparison with others. I think that would apply to me.

Whatever the cause may be, as I have told you, I do not believe I am actually capable in any case of a real contact with the sacraments, but only of the intuition that such a contact is possible. All the more is it impossible for me really to know at present what kind of relationship with them is most suitable for me.

There are times when I am tempted to put myself entirely in your hands and to ask you to decide for me. But, when all is said and done, I cannot do this. I have not the right.

I think that with very important things we do not overcome our obstacles. We look at them fixedly for as long as is necessary until, if they are due to the powers of illusion, they disappear. What I call an obstacle is quite a different thing from the kind of inertia we have to overcome at every step we take in the direction of what is good. I have experience of this inertia. Obstacles are quite another matter. If we want to get over them before they have disappeared, we are in danger of those phenomena of compensation, referred to I think by the Gospel passage about the man from whom one devil had gone out and into whom seven others entered forthwith.

The mere thought that, supposing I were baptized with any sentiments other than those that are fitting, I should ever come to have even a single instant or a single inward movement of regret, such a thought fills me with horror. Even if I were certain that baptism was the absolute condition of salvation, I would not run this risk, even to save my soul. I would choose to abstain from it until I became convinced that I was not running this risk. One only has such a conviction when one thinks that one is acting in obedience. Only obedience is invulnerable for all time.

If I had my eternal salvation placed in front of me on this table, and if I only had to stretch out my hand to take it, I would not put out my hand so long as I had not received the order to do so. At least that is what I like to think. And if instead of my own it were the eternal salvation of all human beings, past, present, and to come, I know I ought to do the same thing. In that case I should mind very much. But if I alone were concerned I almost think I should not greatly mind. For I want nothing else but obedience, obedience itself, in its totality, that is to say even to the Cross.

Yet I have no right to speak thus. In speaking thus I lie. For if I desired this I should obtain it; and in fact it continually comes about that I put off for days and days the fulfillment of obligations, which are obvious duties, which I know to be such, easy and simple to carry out in themselves and important in their possible consequences for others. But it would be too long and uninteresting to tell you about my miserable faults. And it would probably not serve any useful purpose. Except that at all events it would prevent you from making any mistake about me.

Do believe in my very real gratitude. I think you know that this is not just a formula.

SIMONE WEIL

LETTER III

About Her Departure

April 16, 1942

DEAR FATHER,

Unless anything unexpected happens we shall be seeing each other in a week for the last time. I am to leave at the end of the month.

If you could arrange things so that we could have time to talk at our leisure of that choice of texts it would be a good thing. But I suppose that it will not be possible.

I do not in the least wish to leave. I shall leave with anguish. The calculations as to probabilities which decide me are so uncertain that they scarcely give me any support. The thought guiding me, and which has been in my mind for years, so that I dare not dismiss it although there is little chance of carrying it out, is fairly close to the project with which you had the great generosity to help me a few months ago, and which did not succeed.

At bottom, the principal reason that is sending me away is that, given the rate at which things are now moving and the conjunction of circumstances, it seems as though the decision to stay would be an act of personal will on my part. And my greatest desire is to lose not only all will but all personal being.

It seems to me as though something were telling me to go. As I am perfectly sure that this is not just emotion, I am abandoning myself to it.

I hope that this abandonment, even if I am mistaken, will finally bring me to the haven.

What I call the haven, as you know, is the Cross. If it cannot be given me to deserve one day to share the Cross of Christ, at least may I share that of the good thief. Of all the beings other than Christ of whom the Gospel tells us, the good thief is by far the one I most envy. To have been at the side of Christ and in the same state during the crucifixion seems to me a far more enviable privilege than to be at the right hand of his glory.

Although the time is near, I have not yet made my decision quite irrevocably. Therefore, if by chance you have any advice to give me, now is the moment. But do not think about it specially. You have a great many far more important things to think about.

Once I have gone, it seems to me very improbable that circumstances will allow me to see you again one day. As to eventual meetings in another world, you know that I do not picture things to myself in that way. But that does not matter very much. It is enough for my friendship with you that you exist.

I shall not be able to help thinking with keen anguish of all those whom I shall have left in France and of you in particular. But that also does not matter. I think that you are among those to whom, whatever happens, no real harm can ever come.

Distance will not prevent my debt to you from increasing day by day, as time passes. For it will not prevent me from thinking of you. And it is impossible to think of you without thinking of God.

Do believe in my filial friendship.

SIMONE WEIL

P.S. You know that for me there is no question in this departure of an escape from suffering and danger. My anguish comes precisely from the fear that in spite of myself, and unwittingly, by going I shall be doing what I want above everything else not to do—that is to say running away. Up till now we have lived here very peacefully. If this peace is destroyed just after I have gone away, it will be frightful for me. If I were sure it was going to be like that, I think that I should stay. If you know anything that might throw any light on what is going to happen, I count on you to tell me.

LETTER IV

Spiritual Autobiography

P.S. To Be Read First.

This letter is fearfully long—but as there is no question of an answer—especially as I shall doubtless have gone before it reaches you—you have years ahead of you in which to read it if you care to. Read it all the same, one day or another.

From Marseilles, about May 15

Father,

Before leaving I want to speak to you again, it may be the last time perhaps, for over there I shall probably send you only my news from time to time just so as to have yours.

I told you that I owed you an enormous debt. I want to try to tell you exactly what it consists of. I think that if you could really understand what my spiritual state is you would not be at all sorry that you did not lead me to baptism. But I do not know if it is possible for you to understand this.

You neither brought me the Christian inspiration nor did you bring me to Christ; for when I met you there was no

61

longer any need; it had been done without the intervention of any human being. If it had been otherwise, if I had not already been won, not only implicitly but consciously, you would have given me nothing, because I should have received nothing from you. My friendship for you would have been a reason for me to refuse your message, for I should have been afraid of the possibilities of error and illusion which human influence in the divine order is likely to involve.

I may say that never at any moment in my life have I 'sought for God.' For this reason, which is probably too subjective, I do not like this expression and it strikes me as false. As soon as I reached adolescence, I saw the problem of God as a problem the data of which could not be obtained here below, and I decided that the only way of being sure not to reach a wrong solution, which seemed to me the greatest possible evil, was to leave it alone. So I left it alone. I neither affirmed nor denied anything. It seemed to me useless to solve the problem, for I thought that, being in this world, our business was to adopt the best attitude with regard to the problems of this world, and that such an attitude did not depend upon the solution of the problem of God.

This held good as far as I was concerned at any rate, for I never hesitated in my choice of an attitude; I always adopted the Christian attitude as the only possible one. I might say that I was born, I grew up, and I always remained within the Christian inspiration. While the very name of God had no part in my thoughts, with regard to the problems of this world and this life I shared the Christian conception in an explicit and rigorous manner, with the most specific notions it involves. Some of these notions have been part of my outlook for as far back as I can remember. With others I know the time and manner of their coming and the form under which they imposed themselves upon me.

For instance I never allowed myself to think of a future state, but I always believed that the instant of death is the center and object of life. I used to think that, for those who live as they should, it is the instant when, for an infinitesimal fraction of time, pure truth, naked, certain, and eternal enters the soul. I may say that I never desired any other good for myself. I thought that the life leading to this good is not only defined by a code of morals common to all, but that for each one it consists of a succession of acts and events strictly personal to him, and so essential that he who leaves them on one side never reaches the goal. The notion of vocation was like this for me. I saw that the carrying out of a vocation differed from the actions dictated by reason or inclination in that it was due to an impulse of an essentially and manifestly different order; and not to follow such an impulse when it made itself felt, even if it demanded impossibilities, seemed to me the greatest of all ills. Hence my conception of obedience; and I put this conception to the test when I entered the factory and stayed on there, even when I was in that state of intense and uninterrupted misery about which I recently told you. The most beautiful life possible has always seemed to me to be one where everything is determined, either by the pressure of circumstances or by impulses such as I have just mentioned and where there is never any room for choice.

63

At fourteen I fell into one of those fits of bottomless despair that come with adolescence, and I seriously thought of dying because of the mediocrity of my natural faculties. The exceptional gifts of my brother, who had a childhood and youth comparable to those of Pascal, brought my own inferiority home to me. I did not mind having no visible successes, but what did grieve me was the idea of being excluded from that transcendent kingdom to which only the truly great have access and wherein truth abides. I preferred to die rather than live without that truth. After months of inward darkness, I suddenly had the everlasting conviction that any human being, even though practically devoid of natural faculties, can penetrate to the kingdom of truth reserved for genius, if only he longs for truth and perpetually concentrates all his attention upon its attainment. He thus becomes a genius too, even though for lack of talent his genius cannot be visible from outside. Later on, when the strain of headaches caused the feeble faculties I possess to be invaded by a paralysis, which I was quick to imagine as probably incurable, the same conviction led me to persevere for ten years in an effort of concentrated attention that was practically unsupported by any hope of results.

Under the name of truth I also included beauty, virtue, and every kind of goodness, so that for me it was a question of a conception of the relationship between grace and desire. The conviction that had come to me was that when one hungers for bread one does not receive stones. But at that time I had not read the Gospel.

Just as I was certain that desire has in itself an efficacy in the realm of spiritual goodness whatever its form, I thought it was also possible that it might not be effective in any other realm.

As for the spirit of poverty, I do not remember any moment when it was not in me, although only to that unhappily small extent compatible with my imperfection. I fell in love with Saint Francis of Assisi as soon as I came to know about him. I always believed and hoped that one day Fate would force upon me the condition of a vagabond and a beggar which he embraced freely. Actually I felt the same way about prison.

From my earliest childhood I always had also the Christian idea of love for one's neighbor, to which I gave the name of justice—a name it bears in many passages of the Gospel and which is so beautiful. You know that on this point I have failed seriously several times.

The duty of acceptance in all that concerns the will of God, whatever it may be, was impressed upon my mind as the first and most necessary of all duties from the time when I found it set down in Marcus Aurelius under the form of the *amor fati* of the Stoics. I saw it as a duty we cannot fail in without dishonoring ourselves.

The idea of purity, with all that this word can imply for a Christian, took possession of me at the age of sixteen, after a period of several months during which I had been going through the emotional unrest natural in adolescence. This idea came to me when I was contemplating a mountain landscape and little by little it was imposed upon me in an irresistible manner.

Of course I knew quite well that my conception of life was Christian. That is why it never occurred to me that I could enter the Christian community. I had the idea that I was born inside. But to add dogma to this conception of life, without being forced to do so by indisputable evidence, would have seemed to me like a lack of honesty. I should even have thought I was lacking in honesty had I considered the question of the truth of dogma as a problem for myself or even had I simply desired to reach a conclusion on this subject. I have an extremely severe standard for intellectual honesty, so severe that I never met anyone who did not seem to fall short of it in more than one respect; and I am always afraid of failing in it myself.

Keeping away from dogma in this way, I was prevented by a sort of shame from going into churches, though all the same I like being in them. Nevertheless, I had three contacts with Catholicism that really counted.

After my year in the factory, before going back to teaching, I had been taken by my parents to Portugal, and while there I left them to go alone to a little village. I was, as it were, in pieces, soul and body. That contact with affliction * had killed my youth. Until then I had not had any experience of affliction, unless we count my own, which, as it was my own, seemed to me, to have little importance, and which moreover was only a partial affliction, being biological and not social. I knew quite well that there was a great deal of affliction in the world, I was obsessed with the idea, but I had not had prolonged and first-hand experience of it. As I worked in the factory, indistinguishable to all eyes, including my own, from the anonymous mass, the affliction of others entered into my flesh and my soul. Nothing separated

* *Malheur*, see footnote page 117.

me from it, for I had really forgotten my past and I looked forward to no future, finding it difficult to imagine the possibility of surviving all the fatigue. What I went through there marked me in so lasting a manner that still today when any human being, whoever he may be and in whatever circumstances, speaks to me without brutality, I cannot help having the impression that there must be a mistake and that unfortunately the mistake will in all probability disappear. There I received forever the mark of a slave, like the branding of the red-hot iron the Romans put on the foreheads of their most despised slaves. Since then I have always regarded myself as a slave.

In this state of mind then, and in a wretched condition physically, I entered the little Portuguese village, which, alas, was very wretched too, on the very day of the festival of its patron saint. I was alone. It was the evening and there was a full moon over the sea. The wives of the fishermen were, in procession, making a tour of all the ships, carrying candles and singing what must certainly be very ancient hymns of a heart-rending sadness. Nothing can give any idea of it. I have never heard anything so poignant unless it were the song of the boatmen on the Volga. There the conviction was suddenly borne in upon me that Christianity is pre-eminently the religion of slaves, that slaves cannot help belonging to it, and I among others.

In 1937 I had two marvelous days at Assisi. There, alone in the little twelfth-century Romanesque chapel of Santa Maria degli Angeli, an incomparable marvel of purity where Saint Francis often used to pray, something stronger than

I was compelled me for the first time in my life to go down on my knees.

In 1938 I spent ten days at Solesmes, from Palm Sunday to Easter Tuesday, following all the liturgical services. I was suffering from splitting headaches; each sound hurt me like a blow; by an extreme effort of concentration I was able to rise above this wretched flesh, to leave it to suffer by itself, heaped up in a corner, and to find a pure and perfect joy in the unimaginable beauty of the chanting and the words. This experience enabled me by analogy to get a better understanding of the possibility of loving divine love in the midst of affliction. It goes without saying that in the course of these services the thought of the Passion of Christ entered into my being once and for all.

There was a young English Catholic there from whom I gained my first idea of the supernatural power of the sacraments because of the truly angelic radiance with which he seemed to be clothed after going to communion. Chance— for I always prefer saying chance rather than Providence— made of him a messenger to me. For he told me of the existence of those English poets of the seventeenth century who are named metaphysical. In reading them later on, I discovered the poem of which I read you what is unfortunately a very inadequate translation. It is called "Love".* I learned it by heart. Often, at the culminating point of a violent headache, I make myself say it over, concentrating all my attention upon it and clinging with all my soul to the tenderness it enshrines. I used to think I was merely reciting it as a beautiful poem, but without my knowing it the recita-

* By George Herbert. (See introduction, pp. 24-25, for text.)

tion had the virtue of a prayer. It was during one of these recitations that, as I told you, Christ himself came down and took possession of me.

In my arguments about the insolubility of the problem of God I had never foreseen the possibility of that, of a real contact, person to person, here below, between a human being and God. I had vaguely heard tell of things of this kind, but I had never believed in them. In the *Fioretti* the accounts of apparitions rather put me off if anything, like the miracles in the Gospel. Moreover, in this sudden possession of me by Christ, neither my senses nor my imagination had any part; I only felt in the midst of my suffering the presence of a love, like that which one can read in the smile on a beloved face.

I had never read any mystical works because I had never felt any call to read them. In reading as in other things I have always striven to practice obedience. There is nothing more favorable to intellectual progress, for as far as possible I only read what I am hungry for at the moment when I have an appetite for it, and then I do not read, I *eat*. God in his mercy had prevented me from reading the mystics, so that it should be evident to me that I had not invented this absolutely unexpected contact.

Yet I still half refused, not my love but my intelligence. For it seemed to me certain, and I still think so today, that one can never wrestle enough with God if one does so out of pure regard for the truth. Christ likes us to prefer truth to him because, before being Christ, he is truth. If one turns aside from him to go toward the truth, one will not go far before falling into his arms.

After this I came to feel that Plato was a mystic, that all the *Iliad* is bathed in Christian light, and that Dionysus and Osiris are in a certain sense Christ himself; and my love was thereby redoubled.

I never wondered whether Jesus was or was not the Incarnation of God; but in fact I was incapable of thinking of him without thinking of him as God.

In the spring of 1940 I read the *Bhagavad-Gita*. Strange to say it was in reading those marvelous words, words with such a Christian sound, put into the mouth of an incarnation of God, that I came to feel strongly that we owe an allegiance to religious truth which is quite different from the admiration we accord to a beautiful poem; it is something far more categorical.

Yet I did not believe it to be possible for me to consider the question of baptism. I felt that I could not honestly give up my opinions concerning the non-Christian religions and concerning Israel—and as a matter of fact time and meditation have only served to strengthen them—and I thought that this constituted an absolute obstacle. I did not imagine it as possible that a priest could even dream of granting me baptism. If I had not met you, I should never have considered the problem of baptism as a practical problem.

During all this time of spiritual progress I had never prayed. I was afraid of the power of suggestion that is in prayer—the very power for which Pascal recommends it. Pascal's method seems to me one of the worst for attaining faith.

Contact with you was not able to persuade me to pray. On the contrary I thought the danger was all the greater, since I also had to beware of the power of suggestion in my friendship with you. At the same time I found it very difficult not to pray and not to tell you so. Moreover I knew I could not tell you without completely misleading you about myself. At that time I should not have been able to make you understand.

Until last September I had never once prayed in all my life, at least not in the literal sense of the word. I had never said any words to God, either out loud or mentally. I had never pronounced a liturgical prayer. I had occasionally recited the *Salve Regina*, but only as a beautiful poem.

Last summer, doing Greek with T——, I went through the Our Father word for word in Greek. We promised each other to learn it by heart. I do not think he ever did so, but some weeks later, as I was turning over the pages of the Gospel, I said to myself that since I had promised to do this thing and it was good, I ought to do it. I did it. The infinite sweetness of this Greek text so took hold of me that for several days I could not stop myself from saying it over all the time. A week afterward I began the vine harvest. I recited the Our Father in Greek every day before work, and I repeated it very often in the vineyard.

Since that time I have made a practice of saying it through once each morning with absolute attention. If during the recitation my attention wanders or goes to sleep, in the minutest degree, I begin again until I have once succeeded in going through it with absolutely pure attention. Sometimes it comes about that I say it again out of sheer pleasure, but I only do it if I really feel the impulse.

The effect of this practice is extraordinary and surprises

me every time, for, although I experience it each day, it exceeds my expectation at each repetition.

At times the very first words tear my thoughts from my body and transport it to a place outside space where there is neither perspective nor point of view. The infinity of the ordinary expanses of perception is replaced by an infinity to the second or sometimes the third degree. At the same time, filling every part of this infinity of infinity, there is silence, a silence which is not an absence of sound but which is the object of a positive sensation, more positive than that of sound. Noises, if there are any, only reach me after crossing this silence.

Sometimes, also, during this recitation or at other moments, Christ is present with me in person, but his presence is infinitely more real, more moving, more clear than on that first occasion when he took possession of me.

I should never have been able to take it upon myself to tell you all this had it not been for the fact that I am going away. And as I am going more or less with the idea of probable death, I do not believe that I have the right to keep it to myself. For after all, the whole of this matter is not a question concerning me myself. It concerns God. I am really nothing in it all. If one could imagine any possibility of error in God, I should think that it had all happened to me by mistake. But perhaps God likes to use castaway objects, waste, rejects. After all, should the bread of the host be moldy, it would become the Body of Christ just the same after the priest had consecrated it. Only it cannot refuse, while we can disobey. It sometimes seems to me that when I am treated in so merciful a way, every sin on my part must be a mortal sin. And I am constantly committing them.

I have told you that you are like a father and brother at the same time to me. But these words only express an analogy. Perhaps at bottom they only correspond to a feeling of affection, of gratitude and admiration. For as to the spiritual direction of my soul, I think that God himself has taken it in hand from the start and still looks after it.

That does not prevent me from owing you the greatest debt of gratitude that I could ever have incurred toward any human being. This is exactly what it consists of.

First you once said to me at the beginning of our relationship some words that went to the bottom of my soul. You said: "Be very careful, because if you should pass over something important through your own fault it would be a pity."

That made me see intellectual honesty in a new light. Till then I had only thought of it as opposed to faith; your words made me think that perhaps, without my knowing it, there were in me obstacles to the faith, impure obstacles, such as prejudices, habits. I felt that after having said to myself for so many years simply: "Perhaps all that is not true," I ought, without ceasing to say it—I still take care to say it very often now—to join it to the opposite formula, namely: "Perhaps all that is true," and to make them alternate.

At the same time, in making the problem of baptism a practical problem for me, you have forced me to face the whole question of the faith, dogma, and the sacraments, obliging me to consider them closely and at length with the fullest possible attention, making me see them as things toward which I have obligations that I have to discern and perform. I should never have done this otherwise and it is indispensable for me to do it.

But the greatest blessing you have brought me is of another order. In gaining my friendship by your charity (which I have never met anything to equal), you have provided me with a source of the most compelling and pure inspiration that is to be found among human things. For nothing among human things has such power to keep our gaze fixed ever more intensely upon God, than friendship for the friends of God.

Nothing better enables me to measure the breadth of your charity than the fact that you bore with me for so long and with such gentleness. I may seem to be joking, but that is not the case. It is true that you have not the same motives as I have myself (those about which I wrote to you the other day), for feeling hatred and repulsion toward me. But all the same I feel that your patience with me can only spring from a supernatural generosity.

I have not been able to avoid causing you the greatest disappointment it was in my power to cause you. But up to now, although I have often asked myself the question during prayer, during Mass, or in the light of the radiancy that remains in the soul after Mass, I have never once had, even for a moment, the feeling that God wants me to be in the Church. I have never even once had a feeling of uncertainty. I think that at the present time we can finally conclude that he does not want me in the Church. Do not have any regrets about it.

He does not want it so far at least. But unless I am mistaken I should say that it is his will that I should stay outside for the future too, except perhaps at the moment of death. Yet I am always ready to obey any order, whatever it may be. I should joyfully obey the order to go to the very center of hell and to remain there eternally. I do not mean, of course, that I have a preference for orders of this nature. I am not perverse like that.

Christianity should contain all vocations without exception since it is catholic. In consequence the Church should also. But in my eyes Christianity is catholic by right but not in fact. So many things are outside it, so many things that I love and do not want to give up, so many things that God loves, otherwise they would not be in existence. All the immense stretches of past centuries, except the last twenty are among them; all the countries inhabited by colored races; all secular life in the white peoples' countries; in the history of these countries, all the traditions banned as heretical, those of the Manicheans and Albigenses for instance; all those things resulting from the Renaissance, too often degraded but not quite without value.

Christianity being catholic by right but not in fact, I regard it as legitimate on my part to be a member of the Church by right but not in fact, not only for a time, but for my whole life if need be.

But it is not merely legitimate. So long as God does not give me the certainty that he is ordering me to do anything else, I think it is my duty.

I think, and so do you, that our obligation for the next two or three years, an obligation so strict that we can scarcely fail in it without treason, is to show the public the possibility of a truly incarnated Christianity. In all the history now known there has never been a period in which souls have been in such peril as they are today in every part of the globe. The bronze serpent must be lifted up again so that whoever raises his eyes to it may be saved.

But everything is so closely bound up together that Christianity cannot be really incarnated unless it is catholic in the sense that I have just defined. How could it circulate through the flesh of all the nations of Europe if it did not contain absolutely everything in itself? Except of course falsehood. But in everything that exists there is most of the time more truth than falsehood.

Having so intense and so painful a sense of this urgency, I should betray the truth, that is to say the aspect of truth that I see, if I left the point, where I have been since my birth, at the intersection of Christianity and everything that is not Christianity.

I have always remained at this exact point, on the threshold of the Church, without moving, quite still, ἐν ὑπομένη (it is so much more beautiful a word than *patientia!*); only now my heart has been transported, forever, I hope, into the Blessed Sacrament exposed on the altar.

You see that I am very far from the thoughts that H——, with the best of intentions, attributed to me. I am far also from being worried in any way.

If I am sad, it comes primarily from the permanent sadness that destiny has imprinted forever upon my emotions, where the greatest and purest joys can only be superimposed and that at the price of a great effort of attention. It comes also from my miserable and continual sins; and from all the calamities of our time and of all those of all the past centuries.

I think that you should understand why I have always resisted you, if in spite of being a priest you can admit that a genuine vocation might prevent anyone from entering the Church.

Otherwise a barrier of incomprehension will remain between us, whether the error is on my part or on yours. This would grieve me from the point of view of my friendship for you, because in that case the result of all these efforts and desires, called forth by your charity toward me, would be a disappointment for you. Moreover, although it is not my fault, I should not be able to help feeling guilty of ingratitude. For, I repeat, my debt to you is beyond all measure.

I should like to draw your attention to one point. It is that there is an absolutely insurmountable obstacle to the Incarnation of Christianity. It is the use of the two little words *anathema sit.* It is not their existence, but the way they have been employed up till now. It is that also which prevents me from crossing the threshold of the Church. I remain beside all those things that cannot enter the Church, the universal repository, on account of those two little words. I remain beside them all the more because my own intelligence is numbered among them.

The Incarnation of Christianity implies a harmonious solution of the problem of the relations between the individual and the collective. Harmony in the Pythagorean sense; the just balance of contraries. This solution is precisely what men are thirsting for today.

The position of the intelligence is the key to this harmony, because the intelligence is a specifically and rigorously individual thing. This harmony exists wherever the intelligence, remaining in its place, can be exercised without hindrance and can reach the complete fulfillment of its function. That is what Saint Thomas says admirably of all the parts of the soul of Christ, with reference to his sensitiveness to pain during the crucifixion.

The special function of the intelligence requires total liberty, implying the right to deny everything, and allowing of no domination. Wherever it usurps control there is an excess of individualism. Wherever it is hampered or uneasy there is an oppressive collectivism, or several of them.

The Church and the State should punish it, each one in its own way, when it advocates actions of which they disapprove. When it remains in the region of purely theoretical speculation they still have the duty, should occasion arise, to put the public on their guard, by every effective means, against the danger of the practical influence certain speculations might have upon the conduct of life. But whatever these theoretical speculations may be, the Church and the State have no right either to try to stifle them or to inflict any penalty material or moral upon their authors. Notably, they should not be deprived of the sacraments if they desire them. For, whatever they may have said, even if they have publicly denied the existence of God, they may not have committed any sin. In such a case the Church should declare that they are in error, but it should not demand of them anything whatever in the way of a disavowal of what they have said, nor should it deprive them of the Bread of Life.

A collective body is the guardian of dogma; and dogma is an object of contemplation for love, faith, and intelligence, three strictly individual faculties. Hence, almost since the beginning, the individual has been ill at ease in Christianity, and this uneasiness has been notably one of the intelligence. This cannot be denied.

Christ himself who is Truth itself, when he was speaking before an assembly such as a council, did not address it in the same language as he used in an intimate conversation with his well-beloved friend, and no doubt before the Pharisees he might easily have been accused of contradiction and error. For by one of those laws of nature, which God himself respects, since he has willed them from all eternity, there are two languages that are quite distinct although made up of the same words; there is the collective language and there is the individual one. The Comforter whom Christ sends us, the Spirit of truth, speaks one or other of these languages, whichever circumstances demand, and by a necessity of their nature there is not agreement between them.

When genuine friends of God—such as was Eckhart to my way of thinking—repeat words they have heard in secret amidst the silence of the union of love, and these words are in disagreement with the teaching of the Church, it is simply that the language of the market place is not that of the nuptial chamber.

Everybody knows that really intimate conversation is only possible between two or three. As soon as there are six or seven, collective language begins to dominate. That is why it is a complete misinterpretation to apply to the Church the words "Wheresoever two or three are gathered together in my name, there am I in the midst of them." Christ did not say two hundred, or fifty, or ten. He said two or three. He said precisely that he always forms the third in the intimacy of the tête-à-tête.

Christ made promises to the Church, but none of these promises has the force of the expression "Thy Father who seeth in secret." The word of God is the secret word. He who has not heard this word, even if he adheres to all the dogmas taught by the Church, has no contact with truth.

The function of the Church as the collective keeper of dogma is indispensable. She has the right and the duty to punish those who make a clear attack upon her within the specific range of this function, by depriving them of the sacraments.

Thus, although I know practically nothing of this business, I incline to think provisionally that she was right to punish Luther.

But she is guilty of an abuse of power when she claims to force love and intelligence to model their language upon her own. This abuse of power is not of God. It comes from the natural tendency of every form of collectivism, without exception, to abuse power.

The image of the Mystical Body of Christ is very attractive. But I consider the importance given to this image today as one of the most serious signs of our degeneration. For our true dignity is not to be parts of a body, even though it be a mystical one, even though it be that of Christ. It consists

in this, that in the state of perfection, which is the vocation of each one of us, we no longer live in ourselves, but
Christ lives in us; so that through our perfection Christ in
his integrity and in his indivisible unity, becomes in a sense
each one of us, as he is completely in each host. The hosts
are not a *part* of his body.

This present-day importance of the image of the Mystical
Body shows how wretchedly susceptible Christians are to
outside influences. Undoubtedly there is real intoxication
in being a member of the Mystical Body of Christ. But today a great many other mystical bodies, which have not
Christ for their head, produce an intoxication in their members that to my way of thinking is of the same order.

As long as it is through obedience, I find sweetness in my
deprivation of the joy of membership in the Mystical Body
of Christ. For if God is willing to help me, I may thus bear
witness that without this joy one can nevertheless be faithful to Christ unto death. Social enthusiasms have such
power today, they raise people so effectively to the supreme
degree of heroism in suffering and death, that I think it is
as well that a few sheep should remain outside the fold in
order to bear witness that the love of Christ is essentially
something different.

The Church today defends the cause of the indefeasible
rights of the individual against collective oppression, of
liberty of thought against tyranny. But these are causes
readily embraced by those who find themselves momen-
tarily to be the least strong. It is their only way of perhaps
one day becoming the strongest. That is well known.

You may perhaps be offended by this idea. You are not the Church. During the periods of the most atrocious abuse of power committed by the Church, there must have been some priests like you among the others. Your good faith is not a guarantee, even were it shared by all your Order. You cannot foresee what turn things may take.

In order that the present attitude of the Church should be effective and that she should really penetrate like a wedge into social existence, she would have to say openly that she had changed or wished to change. Otherwise who could take her seriously when they remembered the Inquisition? My friendship for you, which I extend through you to all your Order, makes it very painful for me to bring this up. But it existed. After the fall of the Roman Empire, which had been totalitarian, it was the Church that was the first to establish a rough sort of totalitarianism in Europe in the thirteenth century, after the war with the Albigenses. This tree bore much fruit.

And the motive power of this totalitarianism was the use of those two little words: *anathema sit.*

It was moreover by a judicious transposition of this use that all the parties which in our own day have founded totalitarian regimes were shaped. This is a point of history I have specially studied.

I must give you the impression of a Luciferian pride in speaking thus of a great many matters that are too high for me and about which I have no right to understand anything. It is not my fault. Ideas come and settle in my mind by mistake, then, realizing their mistake, they absolutely insist on coming out. I do not know where they come from, or what they are worth, but, whatever the risk, I do not think I have the right to prevent this operation.

Good-by, I wish you all possible good things except the cross; for I do not love my neighbor as myself, you particularly, as you have noticed. But Christ granted to his well-beloved disciple, and probably to all that disciple's spiritual lineage, to come to him not through degradation, defilement, and distress, but in uninterrupted joy, purity, and sweetness. That is why I can allow myself to wish that even if one day you have the honor of dying a violent death for Our Lord, it may be with joy and without any anguish; also that only three of the beatitudes (*mites, mundo corde, pacifici*) will apply to you. All the others involve more or less of suffering.

This wish is not due only to the frailty of human friendship. For, with any human being taken individually, I always find reasons for concluding that sorrow and misfortune do not suit him, either because he seems too mediocre for anything so great or, on the contrary, too precious to be destroyed. One cannot fail more seriously in the second of the two essential commandments. And as to the first, I fail to observe that, in a still more horrible manner, for every time I think of the crucifixion of Christ I commit the sin of envy.

Believe more than ever and forever in my filial and tenderly grateful friendship.

SIMONE WEIL

LETTER V

Her Intellectual Vocation

From Casablanca

DEAR S.,

I am sending you four things.

First a personal letter for Father Perrin. It is very long and contains nothing that cannot wait indefinitely. Do not send it to him; give it to him when you see him and tell him not to read it until one day when he has leisure and liberty of mind.

Secondly (in an envelope that I have sealed for convenience but which you are to open as well as the other two), you will find the commentary of the Pythagorean texts, which I did not have time to finish, and which is to be joined to the work I left with you when I came away. It will be quite easy, because it is numbered. The way it is drawn up and put together is horribly bad; it is certainly very difficult to follow if read aloud and far too long to be copied out. But I can only send it as it is.

Thirdly, I have also enclosed the copy of a translation of a fragment from Sophocles which I found among my papers. It is the whole dialogue between Electra and Orestes of which I had only copied a few verses in the work you have already. As I wrote it out, each word struck the very center of my being with so deep and so secret a resonance that the interpretation of Electra as the human soul and Orestes as Christ is almost as certain for me as if I had written these verses myself. Tell Father Perrin that too. In reading the text he will understand.

Read him also what I am writing you now; I hope from the bottom of my heart that it will not grieve him too much.

In finishing the work on the Pythagoreans, I felt definitively and certainly, as far as a human being has the right to use these two words, that my vocation imposes upon me the necessity of remaining outside the Church, without so much as engaging myself in any way, even implicitly, to her or to the dogmas of Christianity, in any case for as long as I am not quite incapable of intellectual work. And that is in order that I may serve God and the Christian faith in the realm of the intelligence. The degree of intellectual honesty that is obligatory for me, by reason of my particular vocation, demands that my thought should be indifferent to all ideas without exception, including for instance materialism and atheism; it must be equally welcoming and equally reserved with regard to everyone of them. Water is indifferent in this way to the objects that fall into it. It does not weigh them; they weigh themselves, after a certain time of oscillation.

I know quite well that I am not really like this—it would be too beautiful; but I am under an obligation to be like this; and I could never be like this if I were in the Church.

In my particular case, in order to be born of water and the spirit, I must abstain from the visible water.

It is not that I feel within me a capacity for intellectual creation. But I feel obligations that are related to such a creation. It is not my fault. Nobody but myself can appreciate these obligations. The conditions of intellectual or artistic creation are so intimate and secret that no one can penetrate into them from outside. I know that artists excuse their bad actions in this way. But it has to do with something very different in my case.

This indifference of thought on the level of the intelligence is in no way incompatible with the love of God, or even with a vow of love inwardly renewed each second of each day, each time eternal and each time wholly complete and new. I should be like this if I were what I ought to be.

This position may seem to be very unstably balanced, but faithfulness, of which I hope God will not refuse me the grace, makes it possible to remain thus indefinitely without moving ἐν ὑπομένῃ.

It is for the service of Christ as the Truth that I deprive myself of sharing in his flesh in the way he has instituted. He deprives me of it, to be more exact, for never up till now have I had even for a second the impression of there being any choice. I am as certain as a human being has the right to be that I am deprived in this way for my whole life; except perhaps—only perhaps—if circumstances make intellectual work definitively and totally impossible for me.

If this grieves Father Perrin, I can only hope that he may forget me soon; for I would infinitely prefer to have no place in his thoughts than to be the cause of the slightest sorrow to him. Unless by chance he were able to draw some good from it.

To return to my list, I am also sending you the paper on the spiritual employment of school studies, which I had taken away by mistake. That is for Father Perrin too on account of his indirect relations with the *jécistes* * of Montpellier. Anyhow he can do what he likes with it.

Do let me thank you again from the bottom of my heart for your kindness to me. I shall often think of you. I hope that we shall have news of each other from time to time but it is not certain.

Yours affectionately,

SIMONE WEIL

* Members of the J.E.C. (Jeunesse Étudiante Chrétienne). There are also movements known as the J.O.C. (Jeunesse Ouvrière Chrétienne) and the J.A.C. (Jeunesse Agricole Chrétienne).

LETTER VI

Last Thoughts

May 26, 1942
From Casablanca

FATHER,

It was a very kind act on your part to write to me all the same.

I valued having a few affectionate words from you at the moment of leaving.

You quoted some glorious words of Saint Paul. I hope though that in owning my wretchedness to you I did not give you the impression of misunderstanding God's mercy. I hope I have never fallen, and never shall fall, to such a depth of cowardice and ingratitude. I do not need any hope or any promise in order to believe that God is rich in mercy. I know this wealth of his with the certainty of experience; I have touched it. What I know of it through actual contact is so far beyond my capacity of understanding and gratitude that even the promise of future bliss could add nothing to it for me; since for human intelligence the addition of two infinites is not an addition.

God's mercy is manifest in affliction as in joy, by the

88

same right, more perhaps, because under this form it has no human analogy. Man's mercy is only shown in giving joy, or maybe in inflicting pain with a view to outward results, bodily healing or education. But it is not the outward results of affliction that bear witness to divine mercy. The outward results of true affliction are nearly always bad. We lie when we try to disguise this. It is in affliction itself that the splendor of God's mercy shines, from its very depths, in the heart of its inconsolable bitterness. If still persevering in our love, we fall to the point where the soul cannot keep back the cry "My God, why hast thou forsaken me?" if we remain at this point without ceasing to love, we end by touching something that is not affliction, not joy, something that is the central essence, necessary and pure, something not of the senses, common to joy and sorrow: the very love of God.

We know then that joy is the sweetness of contact with the love of God, that affliction is the wound of this same contact when it is painful, and that only the contact matters, not the manner of it.

It is the same as when we see someone very dear to us after a long absence; the words we exchange with him do not matter, but only the sound of his voice, which assures us of his presence.

The knowledge of this presence of God does not afford consolation; it takes nothing from the fearful bitterness of affliction; nor does it heal the mutilation of the soul. But we know quite certainly that God's love for us is the very substance of this bitterness and this mutilation.

89

I should like out of gratitude to be capable of bearing witness to this.

The poet of the *Iliad* loved God enough to have this capacity. This indeed is the implicit signification of the poem and the one source of its beauty. But it has scarcely been understood.

Even if there were nothing more for us than life on earth, even if the instant of death were to bring us nothing new, the infinite superabundance of the divine mercy is already secretly present here below in its entirety.

If, by an absurd hypothesis, I were to die without ever having committed any serious faults and yet all the same I were to fall to the bottom of hell, I should nevertheless owe God an infinite debt of gratitude for his infinite mercy, on account of my earthly life, and that notwithstanding the fact that I am such a poor unsatisfactory creature. Even in this hypothesis I should think all the same that I had received all my share of the riches of divine mercy. For already here below we receive the capacity for loving God and for representing him to ourselves with complete certainty as having the substance of real, eternal, perfect, and infinite joy. Through our fleshly veils we receive from above presages of eternity which are enough to efface all doubts on this subject.

What more can we ask or desire? A mother or a lover who knew for certain that her son, or her beloved, was full of joy would have no thought in her heart capable of asking or desiring anything else. We have much more. What we love is perfect joy itself. When we know this, even hope becomes superfluous; it no longer has any meaning. The only thing left to hope for is the grace not to be disobedient here below. The rest is the affair of God alone and does not concern us.

That is why I lack nothing, although my imagination, mutilated as it is by overlong and uninterrupted suffering, cannot conceive of salvation as of something possible for me. What you say can have no effect except to persuade me that you really have some friendship for me. From that point of view I treasure your letter greatly. It has not been able to affect me in any other way. But that was not necessary.

I know enough of my miserable weakness to suppose that a little adverse fortune would perhaps suffice to fill my soul with suffering to such a point that for a long time no room would be left for the thoughts I have just described to you. But even that does not matter very much. Certitude does not depend upon states of soul. Certitude is always in perfect security.

There is only one time when I really know nothing of this certitude any longer. It is when I am in contact with the affliction of other people, those who are indifferent or unknown to me as much as the others, perhaps even more, including those of the most remote ages of antiquity. This contact causes me such atrocious pain and so utterly rends my soul that as a result the love of God becomes almost impossible for me for a while. It would take very little more to make me say impossible. So much so that I am uneasy about myself. I reassure myself a little by remembering that Christ wept on foreseeing the horrors of the destruction of Jerusalem. I hope he will forgive me my compassion.

You give me pain by writing that the day of my baptism would be a great joy for you. After having received so much from you, it is in my power to cause you joy; and yet it does not enter my head for a second to do so. I cannot help it. I really believe that only God has the power to prevent me from causing you joy.

Even if we only consider the plane of purely human relations, the gratitude I owe you is infinite. I think that, except you, all those human beings for whom I have made it easy to hurt me through my friendship have amused themselves by doing so, frequently or occasionally, consciously or unconsciously, but all of them at some time or another. Where I recognized it to be conscious, I took a knife and cut out the friendship, without however warning the person in question.

They did not behave like this from malice, but as a result of the well-known phenomenon that makes hens rush upon one of their number if it is wounded, attacking and pecking it.

All men bear this animal nature within them. It determines their attitude toward their fellows, with or without their knowledge and consent. Thus it sometimes happens that without the mind realizing anything, the animal nature in a man senses the mutilation of the animal nature in another and reacts accordingly. It is the same for all possible situations and the corresponding animal reactions. This mechanical necessity holds all men in its grip at every moment. They only escape from it in proportion to the place held in their souls by the authentically supernatural.

Even partial discernment is very difficult in this matter.

If, however, it really were completely possible, we should have there a criterion of the part played by the supernatural in the life of a soul, a sure criterion, exact as a balance and quite independent of any religious beliefs. It is that among many other things that Christ indicated when he said: "These two commandments are one."

It is only with you that I have never felt the backlash of this mechanism. My situation with regard to you is like that of a beggar, reduced by extreme poverty to a state of constant hunger, who for the space of a year had been going at intervals to a prosperous house where he was given bread, and who, for the first time in his life had not suffered humiliation. Such a beggar, if he had a whole life to give in exchange for each morsel of bread, and if he gave them all, would think that his debt was in no way diminished.

But the fact that with you human relations perpetually enshrine the light of God should raise gratitude to a still higher degree in my case.

Yet I am not going to give you any signs of gratitude unless it be to say things concerning you that might give you every reason to be irritated with me. For it is no way fitting that I should say them, nor even think them. I have no right to do this, and I am well aware of it.

As, however, it is a fact that I have thought them, I dare not keep them from you. If they are not true they will do no harm. It is not impossible that they contain some truth. In that case there would be good reason to think that God was sending you this truth through the pen I am holding. It is more suitable for some thoughts to come by direct inspiration; it is more suitable for others to be transmitted through some creature. God uses either way with his friends. It is well known that no matter what thing, a donkey for instance, can be used as agent without making any difference. It pleases God perhaps to choose the most worthless objects for this purpose. I am obliged to tell myself these things so as not to be afraid of my own thoughts.

When I let you have a written sketch of my spiritual autobiography, I had a reason. I wanted to make it possible for you to see for yourself a concrete and certain example of implicit faith. Certain, for I knew that you know that I am not lying.

Wrongly or rightly you think that I have a right to the name of Christian. I assure you that when in speaking of my childhood and youth I use the words vocation, obedience, spirit of poverty, purity, acceptance, love of one's neighbor, and other expressions of the same kind, I am giving them the exact signification they have for me now. Yet I was brought up by my parents and my brother in a complete agnosticism, and I never made the slightest effort to depart from it; I never had the slightest desire to do so, quite rightly, I think. In spite of that, ever since my birth, so to speak, not one of my faults, not one of my imperfections really had the excuse of ignorance. I shall have to answer for everything on that day when the Lamb shall come in anger.

You can take my word for it too that Greece, Egypt, ancient India, and ancient China, the beauty of the world, the pure and authentic reflections of this beauty in art and science, what I have seen of the inner recesses of human hearts where religious belief is unknown, all these things have done as much as the visibly Christian ones to deliver me into Christ's hands as his captive. I think I might even say more. The love of those things that are outside visible Christianity keeps me outside the Church.

Such a spiritual destiny must seem unintelligible to you. But for this very reason it provides useful matter for reflection. It is good to reflect about whatever forces us to come out of ourselves. I have difficulty in imagining how it can be that you really have some friendship for me; but as you apparently have, it may be for this purpose.

In theory you fully admit the possibility of implicit faith. In practice also you have a breadth of mind and an intellectual honesty that are very exceptional. Yet they still seem to me very insufficient. Only perfection is sufficient.

Wrongly or rightly I have often thought I could detect a bias in some of your attitudes. Notably a certain unwillingness when it comes to real facts to admit the possibility of implicit faith in particular cases. At least I had that impression in talking to you about B——. And above all about a Spanish peasant whom I regard as being not very far from sanctity. It is true that it was probably my own fault more than anything else; my awkwardness is so great that I always do harm to those I love when I speak of them; I have often experienced this. But it also seems to me that when one speaks to you of unbelievers who are in affliction and accept their affliction as a part of the order of the world, it does not impress you in the same way as if it were a question of Christians and of submission to the will of God. Yet it is the same thing. At any rate if I really have the right to be called a Christian, I know from experience that the virtue of the Stoics and that of the Christians are one and the same virtue. I mean true Stoical virtue of course, which is before anything else love, not the caricature which a few Roman brutes made of it. In theory I do not think that you would be able to deny it either. But, when it comes to facts and to concrete examples from the contemporary world, you dislike recognizing the possibility of Stoical virtue having supernatural efficacity.

You also hurt me very much one day by using the word false when you meant nonorthodox. You corrected yourself immediately. To my mind there is a confusion of terms there which is incompatible with perfect intellectual honesty. It is impossible that such a thing should be pleasing to Christ, who is the Truth.

It seems to me certain that this constitutes a serious imperfection in you. And why should there be any imperfection in you? It does not suit you in the least to be imperfect. It is like a wrong note in a beautiful song.

I believe this imperfection comes from attaching yourself to the Church as to an earthly country. As a matter of fact, as well as being your bond with the heavenly country, it is a terrestrial country for you. You live there in an atmosphere of human warmth. That makes a little attachment almost inevitable.

Such an attachment is perhaps for you that infinitely fine thread, of which Saint John of the Cross speaks, which so long as it is not broken holds the bird down on the ground as effectively as a great metal chain. I imagine that the last thread, although very fine, must be the most difficult to cut, for when it is cut we have to fly and that is frightening. But all the same the obligation is imperative.

The children of God should not have any other country here below but the universe itself, with the totality of all the reasoning creatures it ever has contained, contains, or ever will contain. That is the native city to which we owe our love.

Less vast things than the universe, among them the Church, impose obligations which can be extremely far-reaching. They do not, however, include the obligation to love. At least that is what I believe. I am moreover convinced that no obligation relating to the intelligence is to be found among them either.

Our love should stretch as widely across all space, and should be as equally distributed in every portion of it, as is the very light of the sun. Christ has bidden us to attain to the perfection of our heavenly Father by imitating his indiscriminate bestowal of light. Our intelligence too should have the same complete impartiality.

Every existing thing is equally upheld in its existence by God's creative love. The friends of God should love him to the point of merging their love into his with regard to all things here below.

When a soul has attained a love filling the whole universe indiscriminately, this love becomes the bird with golden wings that pierces an opening in the egg of the world. After that, such a soul loves the universe, not from within but from without; from the dwelling place of the Wisdom of God, our first-born brother. Such a love does not love beings and things in God, but from the abode of God. Being close to God it views all beings and things from there, and its gaze is merged in the gaze of God.

We have to be catholic, that is to say, not bound by so much as a thread to any created thing, unless it be to creation in its totality. Formerly, in the case of the saints, it was possible for this universality to be implicit, even in their own consciousness. They were able implicitly to give the rightful place in their soul, on the one hand to the love due only to God and to all his creation, on the other to their obligations to all that is smaller than the universe. I think that Saint Francis and Saint John of the Cross were like this. That was why they were both poets.

It is true that we have to love our neighbor, but, in the example that Christ gave as an illustration of this commandment, the neighbor is a being of whom nothing is known, lying naked, bleeding, and unconscious on the road. It is a question of completely anonymous, and for that reason, completely universal love.

It is also true that Christ said to his disciples: "Love one another." But I think that there is a question of friendship, a personal friendship between two beings, by which God's friends should be bound each to each. Friendship is the one legitimate exception to the duty of only loving universally. Moreover, to my way of thinking, it is not really pure unless it is so to speak surrounded on all sides by a compact envelope of indifference which preserves a distance.

We are living in times that have no precedent, and in our present situation universality, which could formerly be implicit, has to be fully explicit. It has to permeate our language and the whole of our way of life.

Today it is not nearly enough merely to be a saint, but we must have the saintliness demanded by the present moment, a new saintliness, itself also without precedent.

Maritain said this, but he only enumerated the aspects of saintliness of former days, which, for the time being at least, have become out of date. He did not feel all the miraculous newness the saintliness of today must contain in compensation.

A new type of sanctity is indeed a fresh spring, an invention. If all is kept in proportion and if the order of each thing is preserved, it is almost equivalent to a new revelation of the universe and of human destiny. It is the exposure of a large portion of truth and beauty hitherto concealed under a thick layer of dust. More genius is needed than was needed by Archimedes to invent mechanics and physics. A new saintliness is a still more marvelous invention.

Only a kind of perversity can oblige God's friends to deprive themselves of having genius, since to receive it in superabundance they only need to ask their Father for it in Christ's name.

Such a petition is legitimate, today at any rate, because it is necessary. I think that under this or any equivalent form it is the first thing we have to ask for now; we have to ask for it daily, hourly, as a famished child constantly asks for bread. The world needs saints who have genius, just as a plague-stricken town needs doctors. Where there is a need there is also an obligation.

I cannot make any use of these thoughts, nor of all those that go with them in my mind. In the first place the considerable imperfection I am cowardly enough to leave within myself keeps me at far too great a distance from the point at which they can be put into practice. That is unpardonable on my part. So great a distance, in the best of cases, can only be crossed with the help of time.

But even if I had already crossed it, I am an instrument already rotten. I am too worn out. And even if I believed in the possibility of God's consenting to repair the mutilations of my nature, I could not bring myself to ask it of him. Even if I were sure of his consenting, I could not. Such a request would seem to me an offense against the infinitely tender Love which has made me the gift of affliction.

If no one consents to take any notice of the thoughts that, though I cannot explain why, have settled in so inadequate a being as myself, they will be buried with me. If, as I believe, they contain some truth, it will be a pity. I am prejudicial to them. The fact that they happen to be in me prevents people from paying any attention to them.

I see no one but you whom I can implore to give them your attention. I should like you to transfer the charity you have so generously bestowed from me to that which I bear within me, and which I like to think is of far more value than I am myself.

It is a great sorrow for me to fear that the thoughts that have descended into me should be condemned to death through the contagion of my inadequacy and wretchedness. I never read the story of the barren fig tree without trembling. I think that it is a portrait of me. In it also, nature was powerless, and yet it was not excused. Christ cursed it.

That is why although there are perhaps not any particular, truly serious faults in my life, except those I have owned to you, I think when I consider things in the cold light of reason that I have more just cause to fear God's anger than many a great criminal.

It is not that I actually do fear it. By a strange twist, the thought of God's anger only arouses love in me. It is the thought of the possible favor of God and of his mercy that makes me tremble with a sort of fear.

On the other hand the sense of being like a barren fig tree for Christ tears my heart.

Happily God can quite easily send not only the same thoughts, supposing they are good, but a great many much better ones to somebody who is unblemished and capable of serving him.

But who knows if those I bear in me are not sent, partly at any rate, so that you should make some use of them? They can only be destined for someone who has a little friendship for me, a friendship that is true. Indeed, for other people, in a sense I do not exist. I am the color of dead leaves, like certain unnoticed insects.

Forgive me if in all I have just written to you anything from my pen should strike you as erroneous or out of place. Do not be angry with me.

I do not know whether I shall be able to send you my news or to receive yours in the course of the weeks and months that are to come. But it is only for me that this separation is a misfortune, and therefore, it is not important.

I can only assure you yet again of my filial gratitude and my boundless friendship.

SIMONE WEIL

ESSAYS

Reflections on the Right Use of School Studies with a View to the Love of God

The key to a Christian conception of studies is the realization that prayer consists of attention. It is the orientation of all the attention of which the soul is capable toward God. The quality of the attention counts for much in the quality of the prayer. Warmth of heart cannot make up for it.

The highest part of the attention only makes contact with God, when prayer is intense and pure enough for such a contact to be established; but the whole attention is turned toward God.

Of course school exercises only develop a lower kind of attention. Nevertheless, they are extremely effective in increasing the power of attention that will be available at the time of prayer, on condition that they are carried out with a view to this purpose and this purpose alone.

Although people seem to be unaware of it today, the development of the faculty of attention forms the real object and almost the sole interest of studies. Most school tasks have a certain intrinsic interest as well, but such an interest is secondary. All tasks that really call upon the power of attention are interesting for the same reason and to an almost equal degree.

School children and students who love God should never say: "For my part I like mathematics"; "I like French"; "I like Greek." They should learn to like all these subjects, because all of them develop that faculty of attention which, directed toward God, is the very substance of prayer.

If we have no aptitude or natural taste for geometry, this does not mean that our faculty for attention will not be developed by wrestling with a problem or studying a theorem. On the contrary it is almost an advantage.

It does not even matter much whether we succeed in finding the solution or understanding the proof, although it is important to try really hard to do so. Never in any case whatever is a genuine effort of the attention wasted. It always has its effect on the spiritual plane and in consequence on the lower one of the intelligence, for all spiritual light lightens the mind.

If we concentrate our attention on trying to solve a problem of geometry, and if at the end of an hour we are no nearer to doing so than at the beginning, we have nevertheless been making progress each minute of that hour in another more mysterious dimension. Without our knowing or feeling it, this apparently barren effort has brought more light into the soul. The result will one day be discovered in prayer. Moreover, it may very likely be felt in some department of the intelligence in no way connected with mathematics. Perhaps he who made the unsuccessful effort will one day be able to grasp the beauty of a line of Racine more vividly on account of it. But it is certain that this effort will bear its fruit in prayer. There is no doubt whatever about that.

Certainties of this kind are experimental. But if we do not believe in them before experiencing them, if at least we do not behave as though we believed in them, we shall never have the experience that leads to such certainties. There is a kind of contradiction here. Above a given level this is the case with all useful knowledge concerning spiritual progress. If we do not regulate our conduct by it before having proved it, if we do not hold on to it for a long time by faith alone, a faith at first stormy and without light, we shall never transform it into certainty. Faith is the indispensable condition.

The best support for faith is the guarantee that if we ask our Father for bread, he does not give us a stone. Quite apart from explicit religious belief, every time that a human being succeeds in making an effort of attention with the sole idea of increasing his grasp of truth, he acquires a greater aptitude for grasping it, even if his effort produces no visible fruit. An Eskimo story explains the origin of light as follows: "In the eternal darkness, the crow, unable to find any food, longed for light, and the earth was illumined." If there is a real desire, if the thing desired is really light, the desire for light produces it. There is a real desire when there is an effort of attention. It is really light that is desired if all other incentives are absent. Even if our efforts of attention seem for years to be producing no result, one day a light that is in exact proportion to them will flood the soul. Every effort adds a little gold to a treasure no power on earth can take away. The useless efforts made by the Curé d'Ars, for long and painful years, in his attempt to learn Latin bore fruit in the marvelous discernment that enabled him to see the very soul of his penitents behind their words and even their silences.

Students must therefore work without any wish to gain good marks, to pass examinations, to win school successes; without any reference to their natural abilities and tastes; applying themselves equally to all their tasks, with the idea that each one will help to form in them the habit of that attention which is the substance of prayer. When we set out to do a piece of work, it is necessary to wish to do it correctly, because such a wish is indispensable in any true effort. Underlying this immediate objective, however, our deep purpose should aim solely at increasing the power of attention with a view to prayer; as, when we write, we draw the shape of the letter on paper, not with a view to the shape, but with a view to the idea we want to express. To make this the sole and exclusive purpose of our studies is the first condition to be observed if we are to put them to the right use.

The second condition is to take great pains to examine squarely and to contemplate attentively and slowly each school task in which we have failed, seeing how unpleasing and second rate it is, without seeking any excuse or overlooking any mistake or any of our tutor's corrections, trying to get down to the origin of each fault. There is a great temptation to do the opposite, to give a sideways glance at the corrected exercise if it is bad and to hide it forthwith.

Most of us do this nearly always. We have to withstand this temptation. Incidentally, moreover, nothing is more necessary for academic success, because, despite all our efforts, we work without making much progress when we refuse to give our attention to the faults we have made and our tutor's corrections.

Above all it is thus that we can acquire the virtue of humility, and that is a far more precious treasure than all academic progress. From this point of view it is perhaps even more useful to contemplate our stupidity than our sin. Consciousness of sin gives us the feeling that we are evil, and a kind of pride sometimes finds a place in it. When we force ourselves to fix the gaze, not only of our eyes but of our souls, upon a school exercise in which we have failed through sheer stupidity, a sense of our mediocrity is borne in upon us with irresistible evidence. No knowledge is more to be desired. If we can arrive at knowing this truth with all our souls we shall be well established on the right foundation.

If these two conditions are perfectly carried out there is no doubt that school studies are quite as good a road to sanctity as any other.

To carry out the second, it is enough to wish to do so. This is not the case with the first. In order really to pay attention, it is necessary to know how to set about it.

Most often attention is confused with a kind of muscular effort. If one says to one's pupils: "Now you must pay attention," one sees them contracting their brows, holding their breath, stiffening their muscles. If after two minutes they are asked what they have been paying attention to, they cannot reply. They have been concentrating on nothing. They have not been paying attention. They have been contracting their muscles.

We often expend this kind of muscular effort on our studies. As it ends by making us tired, we have the impression that we have been working. That is an illusion. Tiredness has nothing to do with work. Work itself is the useful effort, whether it is tiring or not. This kind of muscular effort in work is entirely barren, even if it is made with the best of intentions. Good intentions in such cases are among those that pave the way to hell. Studies conducted in such a way can sometimes succeed academically from the point of view of gaining marks and passing examinations, but that is in spite of the effort and thanks to natural gifts; moreover such studies are never of any use.

Will power, the kind that, if need be, makes us set our teeth and endure suffering, is the principal weapon of the apprentice engaged in manual work. But, contrary to the usual belief, it has practically no place in study. The intelligence can only be led by desire. For there to be desire, there must be pleasure and joy in the work. The intelligence only grows and bears fruit in joy. The joy of learning is as indispensable in study as breathing is in running. Where it is lacking there are no real students, but only poor caricatures of apprentices who, at the end of their apprenticeship, will not even have a trade.

It is the part played by joy in our studies that makes of them a preparation for spiritual life, for desire directed toward God is the only power capable of raising the soul. Or rather, it is God alone who comes down and possesses the soul, but desire alone draws God down. He only comes to those who ask him to come; and he cannot refuse to come to those who implore him long, often, and ardently.

Attention is an effort, the greatest of all efforts perhaps, but it is a negative effort. Of itself, it does not involve tiredness. When we become tired, attention is scarcely possible any more, unless we have already had a good deal of practice. It is better to stop working altogether, to seek some relaxation, and then a little later to return to the task; we have to press on and loosen up alternately, just as we breathe in and out.

Twenty minutes of concentrated, untired attention is infinitely better than three hours of the kind of frowning application that leads us to say with a sense of duty done: "I have worked well!"

But, in spite of all appearances, it is also far more difficult. Something in our soul has a far more violent repugnance for true attention than the flesh has for bodily fatigue. This something is much more closely connected with evil than is the flesh. That is why every time that we really concentrate our attention, we destroy the evil in ourselves. If we concentrate with this intention, a quarter of an hour of attention is better than a great many good works.

Attention consists of suspending our thought, leaving it detached, empty, and ready to be penetrated by the object; it means holding in our minds, within reach of this thought, but on a lower level and not in contact with it, the diverse knowledge we have acquired which we are forced to make use of. Our thought should be in relation to all particular and already formulated thoughts, as a man on a mountain who, as he looks forward, sees also below him, without actually looking at them, a great many forests and plains. Above all our thought should be empty, waiting, not seeking anything, but ready to receive in its naked truth the object that is to penetrate it.

All wrong translations, all absurdities in geometry problems, all clumsiness of style, and all faulty connection of ideas in compositions and essays, all such things are due to the fact that thought has seized upon some idea too hastily, and being thus prematurely blocked, is not open to the truth. The cause is always that we have wanted to be too active; we have wanted to carry out a search. This can be proved every time, for every fault, if we trace it to its root. There is no better exercise than such a tracing down of our faults, for this truth is one to be believed only when we have experienced it hundreds and thousands of times. This is the way with all essential truths.

We do not obtain the most precious gifts by going in search of them but by waiting for them. Man cannot discover them by his own powers, and if he sets out to seek for them he will find in their place counterfeits of which he will be unable to discern the falsity.

The solution of a geometry problem does not in itself constitute a precious gift, but the same law applies to it because it is the image of something precious. Being a little fragment of particular truth, it is a pure image of the unique, eternal, and living Truth, the very Truth that once in a human voice declared: "I am the Truth."

Every school exercise, thought of in this way, is like a sacrament.

In every school exercise there is a special way of waiting upon truth, setting our hearts upon it, yet not allowing ourselves to go out in search of it. There is a way of giving our attention to the data of a problem in geometry without trying to find the solution or to the words of a Latin or Greek text without trying to arrive at the meaning, a way of waiting, when we are writing, for the right word to come of itself at the end of our pen, while we merely reject all inadequate words.

Our first duty toward school children and students is to make known this method to them, not only in a general way but in the particular form that bears on each exercise. It is not only the duty of those who teach them but also of their spiritual guides. Moreover the latter should bring out in a brilliantly clear light the correspondence between the attitude of the intelligence in each one of these exercises and the position of the soul, which, with its lamp well filled with oil, awaits the Bridegroom's coming with confidence and desire. May each loving adolescent, as he works at his Latin prose, hope through this prose to come a little nearer to the instant when he will really be the slave—faithfully waiting while the master is absent, watching and listening—ready to open the door to him as soon as he knocks. The master will then make his slave sit down and himself serve him with meat.

Only this waiting, this attention, can move the master to treat his slave with such amazing tenderness. When the slave has worn himself out in the fields, his master says on his return, "Prepare my meal, and wait upon me." And he considers the servant who only does what he is told to do to be unprofitable. To be sure in the realm of action we have to do all that is demanded of us, no matter what effort, weariness, and suffering it may cost, for he who disobeys does not love; but after that we are only unprofitable servants. Such service is a condition of love, but it is not enough. What forces the master to make himself the slave of his slave, and to love him, has nothing to do with all that. Still less is it the result of a search the servant might have been bold enough to undertake on his own initiative. It is only watching, waiting, attention.

Happy then are those who pass their adolescence and youth in developing this power of attention. No doubt they are no nearer to goodness than their brothers working in fields and factories. They are near in a different way. Peasants and workmen possess a nearness to God of incomparable savor which is found in the depths of poverty, in the absence of social consideration and in the endurance of long drawn-out sufferings. If, however, we consider the occupations in themselves, studies are nearer to God because of the attention which is their soul. Whoever goes through years of study without developing this attention within himself has lost a great treasure.

Not only does the love of God have attention for its substance; the love of our neighbor, which we know to be the same love, is made of this same substance. Those who are unhappy have no need for anything in this world but people capable of giving them their attention. The capacity to give one's attention to a sufferer is a very rare and difficult thing; it is almost a miracle; it *is* a miracle. Nearly all those who think they have this capacity do not possess it. Warmth of heart, impulsiveness, pity are not enough.

In the first legend of the Grail, it is said that the Grail (the miraculous vessel * that satisfies all hunger by virtue of the consecrated Host) belongs to the first comer who asks the guardian of the vessel, a king three-quarters paralyzed by the most painful wound, "What are you going through?"

The love of our neighbor in all its fullness simply means being able to say to him: "What are you going through?" It is a recognition that the sufferer exists, not only as a unit in a collection, or a specimen from the social category labeled "unfortunate," but as a man, exactly like us, who was one day stamped with a special mark by affliction. For this reason it is enough, but it is indispensable, to know how to look at him in a certain way.

This way of looking is first of all attentive. The soul empties itself of all its own contents in order to receive into itself the being it is looking at, just as he is, in all his truth. 2- being

Only he who is capable of attention can do this. where peple

So it comes about that, paradoxical as it may seem, a Latin are. prose or a geometry problem, even though they are done wrong, may be of great service one day, provided we devote the right kind of effort to them. Should the occasion arise, they can one day make us better able to give someone in affliction exactly the help required to save him, at the supreme moment of his need.

For an adolescent, capable of grasping this truth and generous enough to desire this fruit above all others, studies

* According to some legends the Grail was made of a single stone, in color like an emerald.

could have their fullest spiritual effect, quite apart from any particular religious belief.

Academic work is one of those fields containing a pearl so precious that it is worth while to sell all our possessions, keeping nothing for ourselves, in order to be able to acquire it.

The Love of God and Affliction*

In the realm of suffering, affliction is something apart, specific, and irreducible. It is quite a different thing from simple suffering. It takes possession of the soul and marks it through and through with its own particular mark, the mark of slavery. Slavery as practiced by ancient Rome is only an extreme form of affliction. The men of antiquity, who knew all about this question, used to say: "A man loses half his soul the day he becomes a slave."

Affliction is inseparable from physical suffering and yet quite distinct. With suffering, all that is not bound up with physical pain or something analogous is artificial, imaginary, and can be eliminated by a suitable adjustment of the mind. Even in the case of the absence or death of someone we love, the irreducible part of the sorrow is akin to physical pain, a difficulty in breathing, a constriction of the heart, an unsatisfied need, hunger, or the almost biological disorder caused by the brutal liberation of some energy, hitherto

*No English word exactly conveys the meaning of the French *malheur*. Our word *unhappiness* is a negative term and far too weak. Affliction is the nearest equivalent but not quite satisfactory. *Malheur* has in it a sense of inevitability and doom.

117

directed by an attachment and now left without a guide. A sorrow that is not centered around an irreducible core of such a nature is mere romanticism or literature. Humiliation is also a violent condition of the whole corporal being, which longs to surge up under the outrage but is forced, by impotence or fear, to hold itself in check.

On the other hand pain that is only physical is a very unimportant matter and leaves no trace in the soul. Toothache is an example. An hour or two of violent pain caused by a decayed tooth is nothing once it is over.

It is another matter if the physical suffering is very prolonged or frequent, but in such a case we are dealing with something quite different from an attack of pain; it is often an affliction.

Affliction is an uprooting of life, a more or less attenuated equivalent of death, made irresistibly present to the soul by the attack or immediate apprehension of physical pain. If there is complete absence of physical pain there is no affliction for the soul, because our thoughts can turn to any object. Thought flies from affliction as promptly and irresistibly as an animal flies from death. Here below, physical pain, and that alone, has the power to chain down our thoughts; on condition that we count as physical pain certain phenomena that, though difficult to describe, are bodily and exactly equivalent to it. Fear of physical pain is a notable example.

When thought is obliged by an attack of physical pain, however slight, to recognize the presence of affliction, a state of mind is brought about, as acute as that of a condemned man who is forced to look for hours at the guillotine that is going to cut off his head. Human beings can live for twenty or fifty years in this acute state. We pass quite close to them without realizing it. What man is capable of discerning such souls unless Christ himself looks through his eyes? We only notice that they have rather a strange way of behaving and we censure this behavior. ⟵ YES!

There is not real affliction unless the event that has seized and uprooted a life attacks it, directly or indirectly, in all its parts, social, psychological, and physical. The social factor is essential. There is not really affliction unless there is social degradation or the fear of it in some form or another.

There is both continuity and the separation of a definite point of entry, as with the temperature at which water boils, between affliction itself and all the sorrows that, even though they may be very violent, very deep and very lasting, are not affliction in the strict sense. There is a limit; on the far side of it we have affliction but not on the near side. This limit is not purely objective; all sorts of personal factors have to be taken into account. The same event may plunge one human being into affliction and not another.

The great enigma of human life is not suffering but affliction. It is not surprising that the innocent are killed, tortured, driven from their country, made destitute, or reduced to slavery, imprisoned in camps or cells, since there are criminals to perform such actions. It is not surprising either that disease is the cause of long sufferings, which paralyze life and make it into an image of death, since nature is at the mercy of the blind play of mechanical necessities. But it *is* surprising that God should have given affliction the power to seize the very souls of the innocent and to take possession

The affliction is aholistic suffering in the suffering. It cuts to the core.

of them as their sovereign lord. At the very best, he who is branded by affliction will keep only half his soul.

As for those who have been struck by one of those blows that leave a being struggling on the ground like a half-crushed worm, they have no words to express what is happening to them. Among the people they meet, those who have never had contact with affliction in its true sense can have no idea of what it is, even though they may have suffered a great deal. Affliction is something specific and impossible to describe in any other terms, as sounds are to anyone who is deaf and dumb. And as for those who have themselves been mutilated by affliction, they are in no state to help anyone at all, and they are almost incapable of even wishing to do so. Thus compassion for the afflicted is an impossibility. When it is really found we have a more astounding miracle than walking on water, healing the sick, or even raising the dead.

YES!

Affliction constrained Christ to implore that he might be spared, to seek consolation from man, to believe he was forsaken by the Father. It forced a just man to cry out against God, a just man as perfect as human nature can be, more so, perhaps, if Job is less a historical character than a figure of Christ. "He laughs at the affliction of the innocent!" This is not blasphemy but a genuine cry of anguish. The Book of Job is a pure marvel of truth and authenticity from beginning to end. As regards affliction, all that departs from this model is more or less stained with falsehood.

Affliction makes God appear to be absent for a time, more absent than a dead man, more absent than light in the utter darkness of a cell. A kind of horror submerges the whole soul. During this absence there is nothing to love. What is terrible is that if, in this darkness where there is nothing to love, the soul ceases to love, God's absence becomes final. The soul has to go on loving in the emptiness, or at least to go on wanting to love, though it may only be with an infinitesimal part of itself. Then, one day, God will come to show himself to this soul and to reveal the beauty of the world to it, as in the case of Job. But if the soul stops loving it falls, even in this life, into something almost equivalent to hell.

That is why those who plunge men into affliction before they are prepared to receive it kill their souls. On the other hand, in a time such as ours, where affliction is hanging over us all, help given to souls is effective only if it goes far enough really to prepare them for affliction. That is no small thing.

Affliction hardens and discourages us because, like a red hot iron, it stamps the soul to its very depths with the scorn, the disgust, and even the self-hatred and sense of guilt and defilement that crime logically should produce but actually does not. Evil dwells in the heart of the criminal without being felt there. It is felt in the heart of the man who is afflicted and innocent. Everything happens as though the state of soul suitable for criminals had been separated from crime and attached to affliction; and it even seems to be in proportion to the innocence of those who are afflicted.

If Job cries out that he is innocent in such despairing accents, it is because he himself is beginning not to believe in it; it is because his soul within him is taking the side of his friends. He implores God himself to bear witness, because he no longer hears the testimony of his own conscience; it is no longer anything but an abstract, lifeless memory for him.

Men have the same carnal nature as animals. If a hen is hurt, the others rush upon it, attacking it with their beaks. This phenomenon is as automatic as gravitation. Our senses attach all the scorn, all the revulsion, all the hatred that our reason attaches to crime, to affliction. Except for those whose whole soul is inhabited by Christ, everybody despises the afflicted to some extent, although practically no one is conscious of it.

This law of sensibility also holds good with regard to ourselves. In the case of someone in affliction, all the scorn, revulsion, and hatred are turned inward. They penetrate to the center of the soul and from there color the whole universe with their poisoned light. Supernatural love, if it has survived, can prevent this second result from coming about, but not the first. The first is of the very essence of affliction; there is no affliction without it.

Christ . . . being made a curse for us. It was not only the body of Christ, hanging on the wood, that was accursed; it was his whole soul also. In the same way every innocent being in his affliction feels himself accursed. This even goes on being true for those who have been in affliction and have come out of it, through a change in their fortunes, that is to say, if the affliction ate deeply enough into them.

Another effect of affliction is, little by little, to make the soul its accomplice, by injecting a poison of inertia into it. In anyone who has suffered affliction for a long enough time there is a complicity with regard to his own affliction. This complicity impedes all the efforts he might make to improve his lot; it goes so far as to prevent him from seeking a way of deliverance, sometimes even to the point of preventing him from wishing for deliverance. Then he is established in affliction, and people might think he was satisfied. Further, this complicity may even induce him to shun the means of deliverance. In such cases it veils itself with excuses which are often ridiculous. Even a person who has come through his affliction will still have something left in him compelling him to plunge into it again, if it has bitten deeply and forever into the substance of his soul. It is as though affliction had established itself in him like a parasite and were directing him to suit its own purposes. Sometimes this impulse triumphs over all the movements of the soul toward happiness. If the affliction has been ended as a result of some kindness, it may take the form of hatred for the benefactor; such is the cause of certain apparently inexplicable acts of savage ingratitude. It is sometimes easy to deliver an unhappy man from his present distress, but it is difficult to set him free from his past affliction. Only God can do it. And even the grace of God itself cannot cure irremediably wounded nature here below. The glorified body of Christ bore the marks of the nails and spear.

One can only accept the existence of affliction by considering it at a distance.

God created through love and for love. God did not create anything except love itself, and the means to love. He created love in all its forms. He created beings capable of love from all possible distances. Because no other could do it, he himself went to the greatest possible distance, the infinite distance. This infinite distance between God and

God, this supreme tearing apart, this agony beyond all others, this marvel of love, is the crucifixion. Nothing can be further from God than that which has been made accursed.

This tearing apart, over which supreme love places the bond of supreme union, echoes perpetually across the universe in the midst of the silence, like two notes, separate yet melting into one, like pure and heart-rending harmony. This is the Word of God. The whole creation is nothing but its vibration. When human music in its greatest purity pierces our soul, this is what we hear through it. When we have learned to hear the silence, this is what we grasp more distinctly through it.

Those who persevere in love hear this note from the very lowest depths into which affliction has thrust them. From that moment they can no longer have any doubt.

Men struck down by affliction are at the foot of the Cross, almost at the greatest possible distance from God. It must not be thought that sin is a greater distance. Sin is not a distance, it is a turning of our gaze in the wrong direction.

It is true that there is a mysterious connection between this distance and an original disobedience. From the beginning, we are told, humanity turned its gaze away from God and walked in the wrong direction for as far as it could go. That was because it could walk then. As for us, we are nailed down to the spot, only free to choose which way we look, ruled by necessity. A blind mechanism, heedless of degrees of spiritual perfection, continually tosses men about and throws some of them at the very foot of the Cross. It rests with them to keep or not to keep their eyes turned

124

toward God through all the jolting. It does not mean that God's Providence is lacking. It is in his Providence that God has willed that necessity should be like a blind mechanism.

If the mechanism were not blind there would not be any affliction. Affliction is <u>anonymous before all things</u>; it deprives its victims of their personality and makes them into things. It is indifferent; and it is the coldness of this indifference—a metallic coldness—that freezes all those it touches right to the depths of their souls. They will never find warmth again. They will never believe any more that they are anyone.

Affliction would not have this power without the element of chance contained by it. <u>Those who are persecuted for their faith and are aware of the fact are not afflicted</u>, although they have to suffer. They only fall into a state of affliction if suffering or fear fills the soul to the point of making it forget the cause of the persecution. The martyrs who entered the arena, singing as they went to face the wild beasts, were not afflicted. Christ was afflicted. He did not die like a martyr. He died like a common criminal, confused with thieves, only a little more ridiculous. For affliction is ridiculous.

Only blind necessity can throw men to the extreme point of distance, right next to the Cross. Human crime, which is the cause of most affliction, is part of blind necessity, because criminals do not know what they are doing.

There are two forms of friendship: meeting and separation. They are indissoluble. Both of them contain some good, and this good of friendship is unique, for when two beings who are not friends are near each other there is no meeting, and when friends are far apart there is no separation. As both forms contain the same good thing, they are both equally good.

God produces himself and knows himself perfectly, just as we in our miserable fashion make and know objects outside ourselves. But, before all things, God is love. Before all things God loves himself. This love, this friendship of God, is the Trinity. Between the terms united by this relation of divine love there is more than nearness; there is infinite nearness or identity. But, resulting from the Creation, the Incarnation, and the Passion, there is also infinite distance. The totality of space and the totality of time, interposing their immensity, put an infinite distance between God and God.

Lovers or friends desire two things. The one is to love each other so much that they enter into each other and only make one being. The other is to love each other so much that, with half the globe between them, their union will not be diminished in the slightest degree. All that man vainly desires here below is perfectly realized in God. We have all those impossible desires within us as a mark of our destination, and they are good for us when we no longer hope to accomplish them.

The love between God and God, which in itself *is* God, is this bond of double virtue: the bond that unites two beings so closely that they are no longer distinguishable and really form a single unity and the bond that stretches across distance and triumphs over infinite separation. The unity of God, wherein all plurality disappears, and the abandonment, wherein Christ believes he is left while never ceasing to love his Father perfectly, these are two forms expressing the divine virtue of the same Love, the Love that is God himself.

God is so essentially love that the unity, which in a sense is his actual definition, is the pure effect of love. Moreover, corresponding to the infinite virtue of unification belonging to this love, there is the infinite separation over which it triumphs, which is the whole creation spread throughout the totality of space and time, made of mechanically harsh matter and interposed between Christ and his Father.

As for us men, our misery gives us the infinitely precious privilege of sharing in this distance placed between the Son and his Father. This distance is only separation, however, for those who love. For those who love, separation, although painful, is a good, because it is love. Even the distress of the abandoned Christ is a good. There cannot be a greater good for us on earth than to share in it. God can never be perfectly present to us here below on account of our flesh. But he can be almost perfectly absent from us in extreme affliction. This is the only possibility of perfection for us on earth. That is why the Cross is our only hope. "No forest bears such a tree, with such blossoms, such foliage, and such fruit."

This universe where we are living, and of which we form a tiny particle, is the distance put by Love between God and God. We are a point in this distance. Space, time, and the mechanism that governs matter are the distance. Everything that we call evil is only this mechanism. God has provided that when his grace penetrates to the very center of a man and from there illuminates all his being, he is able to walk on the water without violating any of the laws of nature.

When, however, a man turns away from God, he simply gives himself up to the law of gravity. Then he thinks that he can decide and choose, but he is only a thing, a stone that falls. If we examine human society and souls closely and with real attention, we see that wherever the virtue of supernatural light is absent, everything is obedient to mechanical laws as blind and as exact as the laws of gravitation. To know this is profitable and necessary. Those whom we call criminals are only tiles blown off a roof by the wind and falling at random. Their only fault is the initial choice by which they became such tiles.

The mechanism of necessity can be transposed to any level while still remaining true to itself. It is the same in the world of pure matter, in the animal world, among nations, and in souls. Seen from our present standpoint, and in human perspective, it is quite blind. If, however, we transport our hearts beyond ourselves, beyond the universe, beyond space and time to where our Father dwells, and if from there we behold this mechanism, it appears quite different. What seemed to be necessity becomes obedience. Matter is entirely passive and in consequence entirely obedient to God's will. It is a perfect model for us. There cannot be any being other than God and that which obeys God. On account of its perfect obedience, matter deserves to be loved by those who love its Master, in the same way as a needle, handled by the beloved wife he has lost, is cherished by a lover. The beauty of the world gives us an intimation of its claim to a place in our heart. In the beauty of the world brute necessity becomes an object of love. What is more beautiful than the action of gravity on the fugitive

128

folds of the sea waves, or on the almost eternal folds of the mountains?

The sea is not less beautiful in our eyes because we know that sometimes ships are wrecked by it. On the contrary, this adds to its beauty. If it altered the movement of its waves to spare a boat, it would be a creature gifted with discernment and choice and not this fluid, perfectly obedient to every external pressure. It is this perfect obedience that constitutes the sea's beauty.

All the horrors produced in this world are like the folds imposed upon the waves by gravity. That is why they contain an element of beauty. Sometimes a poem, such as the *Iliad*, brings this beauty to light.

Men can never escape from obedience to God. A creature cannot but obey. The only choice given to men, as intelligent and <u>free creatures</u>, is to desire obedience or not to desire it. If a man does not desire it, he obeys nevertheless, perpetually, inasmuch as he is a thing subject to mechanical necessity. If he desires it, he is still subject to mechanical necessity, but a new necessity is added to it, a necessity constituted by laws belonging to supernatural things. Certain actions become impossible for him; others are done by his agency, sometimes almost in spite of himself.

When we have the feeling that on some occasion we have disobeyed God, it simply means that for a time we have ceased to desire obedience. Of course it must be understood that, where everything else is equal, a man does not perform the same actions if he gives his consent to obedience as if he does not; just as a plant, where everything else is equal, does not grow in the same way in the light as in the dark.

The plant does not have any control or choice in the matter of its own growth. As for us, we are like plants that have the one choice of being in or out of the light.

Christ proposed the docility of matter to us as a model when he told us to consider the lilies of the field that neither toil nor spin. This means that they have not set out to clothe themselves in this or that color; they have not exercised their will or made arrangements to bring about their object; they have received all that natural necessity brought them. If they appear to be infinitely more beautiful than the richest stuffs, it is not because they are richer but a result of their docility. Materials are docile too, but docile to man, not to God. Matter is not beautiful when it obeys man, but only when it obeys God. If sometimes a work of art seems almost as beautiful as the sea, the mountains, or flowers, it is because the light of God has filled the artist. In order to find things beautiful which are manufactured by men uninspired by God, it would be necessary for us to have understood with our whole soul that these men themselves are only matter, capable of obedience without knowledge. For anyone who has arrived at this point, absolutely everything here below is perfectly beautiful. In everything that exists, in everything that comes about, he discerns the mechanism of necessity, and he appreciates in necessity the infinite sweetness of obedience. For us, this obedience of things in relation to God is what the transparency of a window pane is in relation to light. As soon as we feel this obedience with our whole being, we see God.

When we hold a newspaper upside down, we see the strange shapes of the printed characters. When we turn it the right way up, we no longer see the characters, we see words. The passenger on board a boat caught in a storm feels each jolt as an inward upheaval. The captain is only aware of the complex combination of the wind, the current, and the swell, with the position of the boat, its shape, its sails, its rudder.

As one has to learn to read or to practice a trade, so one must learn to feel in all things, first and almost solely, the obedience of the universe to God. It is really an apprenticeship. Like every apprenticeship, it requires time and effort. He who has reached the end of his training realizes that the differences between things or between events are no more important than those recognized by someone who knows how to read, when he has before him the same sentence reproduced several times, written in red ink and blue, and printed in this, that, or the other kind of lettering. He who does not know how to read only sees the differences. For him who knows how to read, it all comes to the same thing, since the sentence is identical. Whoever has finished his apprenticeship recognizes things and events, everywhere and always, as vibrations of the same divine and infinitely sweet word. This does not mean that he will not suffer. Pain is the color of certain events. When a man who can and a man who cannot read look at a sentence written in red ink, they both see the same red color, but this color is not so important for the one as for the other.

When an apprentice gets hurt, or complains of being tired, the workmen and peasants have this fine expression: "It is the trade entering his body." Each time that we have some pain to go through, we can say to ourselves quite truly

131

Evil can be beautiful depending on how you see it. NO.

that it is the universe, the order, and beauty of the world and the obedience of creation to God that are entering our body. After that how can we fail to bless with tenderest gratitude the Love that sends us this gift?

Joy and suffering are two equally precious gifts both of which must be savored to the full, each one in its purity, without trying to mix them. Through joy, the beauty of the world penetrates our soul. Through suffering it penetrates our body. We could no more become friends of God through joy alone than one becomes a ship's captain by studying books on navigation. The body plays a part in all apprenticeships. On the plane of physical sensibility, suffering alone gives us contact with that necessity which constitutes the order of the world, for pleasure does not involve an impression of necessity. It is a higher kind of sensibility, capable of recognizing a necessity in joy, and that only indirectly through a sense of beauty. In order that our being should one day become wholly sensitive in every part to this obedience that is the substance of matter, in order that a new sense should be formed in us to enable us to hear the universe as the vibration of the word of God, the transforming power of suffering and of joy are equally indispensable. When either of them comes to us we have to open the very center of our soul to it, just as a woman opens her door to messengers from her loved one. What does it matter to a lover if the messenger be polite or rough, so long as he delivers the message?

But affliction is not suffering. Affliction is something quite distinct from a method of God's teaching.

The infinity of space and time separates us from God.

How are we to seek for him? How are we to go toward him? Even if we were to walk for hundreds of years, we should do no more than go round and round the world. Even in an airplane we could not do anything else. We are incapable of progressing vertically. We cannot take a step toward the heavens. God crosses the universe and comes to us.

Over the infinity of space and time, the infinitely more infinite love of God comes to possess us. He comes at his own time. We have the power to consent to receive him or to refuse. If we remain deaf, he comes back again and again like a beggar, but also, like a beggar, one day he stops coming. If we consent, God puts a little seed in us and he goes away again. From that moment God has no more to do; neither have we, except to wait. We only have not to regret the consent we gave him, the nuptial yes. It is not as easy as it seems, for the growth of the seed within us is painful. Moreover, from the very fact that we accept this growth, we cannot avoid destroying whatever gets in its way, pulling up the weeds, cutting the good grass, and unfortunately the good grass is part of our very flesh, so that this gardening amounts to a violent operation. On the whole, however, the seed grows of itself. A day comes when the soul belongs to God, when it not only consents to love but when truly and effectively it loves. Then in its turn it must cross the universe to go to God. The soul does not love like a creature with created love. The love within it is divine, uncreated; for it is the love of God for God that is passing through it. God alone is capable of loving God. We can only consent to give up our own feelings so as to allow free passage in

133

our soul for this love. That is the meaning of denying one-self. We are created for this consent, and for this alone.

Divine Love crossed the infinity of space and time to come from God to us. But how can it repeat the journey in the opposite direction, starting from a finite creature? When the seed of divine love placed in us has grown and become a tree, how can we, we who bear it, take it back to its origin? How can we repeat the journey made by God when he came to us, in the opposite direction? How can we cross infinite distance?

It seems impossible, but there is a way—a way with which we are familiar. We know quite well in what likeness this tree is made, this tree that has grown within us, this most beautiful tree where the birds of the air come and perch. We know what is the most beautiful of all trees. "No forest bears its equal." Something still a little more frightful than a gibbet—that is the most beautiful of all trees. It was the seed of this tree that God placed within us, without our knowing what seed it was. If we had known, we should not have said yes at the first moment. It is this tree that has grown within us and has become ineradicable. Only a be-trayal could uproot it.

When we hit a nail with a hammer, the whole of the shock received by the large head of the nail passes into the point without any of it being lost, although it is only a point. If the hammer and the head of the nail were infinitely big it would be just the same. The point of the nail would trans-mit this infinite shock at the point to which it was applied.

Extreme affliction, which means physical pain, distress of soul, and social degradation, all at the same time, is a nail whose point is applied at the very center of the soul, whose head is all necessity spreading throughout space and time.

Affliction is a marvel of divine technique. It is a simple and ingenious device which introduces into the soul of a finite creature the immensity of force, blind, brutal, and cold. The infinite distance separating God from the creature is entirely concentrated into one point to pierce the soul in its center.

The man to whom such a thing happens has no part in the operation. He struggles like a butterfly pinned alive into an album. But through all the horror he can continue to want to love. There is nothing impossible in that, no obstacle, one might almost say no difficulty. For the greatest suffering, so long as it does not cause the soul to faint, does not touch the acquiescent part of the soul, consenting to a right direction.

It is only necessary to know that love is a direction and not a state of the soul. If one is unaware of this, one falls into despair at the first onslaught of affliction.

He whose soul remains ever turned toward God though the nail pierces it finds himself nailed to the very center of the universe. It is the true center; it is not in the middle; it is beyond space and time; it is God. In a dimension that does not belong to space, that is not time, that is indeed quite a different dimension, this nail has pierced cleanly through all creation, through the thickness of the screen separating the soul from God.

In this marvelous dimension, the soul, without leaving the place and the instant where the body to which it is united is situated, can cross the totality of space and time and come into the very presence of God.

It is at the intersection of creation and its Creator. This point of intersection is the point of intersection of the arms of the Cross.

Saint Paul was perhaps thinking about things of this kind when he said: "That ye, being rooted and grounded in love, may be able to comprehend with all saints what is the breadth, and length, and depth, and height; and to know the love of Christ, which passeth knowledge." *

* Epistle to the Ephesians 3:17-19.

Forms of the Implicit Love of God

Since the commandment "Thou shalt love the Lord thy God" is laid upon us so imperatively, it is to be inferred that the love in question is not only the love a soul can give or refuse when God comes in person to take the hand of his future bride, but also a love preceding this visit, for a permanent obligation is implied.

This previous love cannot have God for its object, since God is not present to the soul and has never yet been so. It must then have another object. Yet it is destined to become the love of God. We can call it the indirect or implicit love of God.

This holds good even when the object of such love bears the name of God, for we can then say either that the name is wrongly applied or that the use of it is permissible only on account of the development bound to follow later.

The implicit love of God can have only three immediate objects, the only three things here below in which God is really though secretly present. These are religious ceremonies, the beauty of the world, and our neighbor. Accordingly there are three loves.

To these three loves friendship should perhaps be added; strictly speaking it is distinct from the love of our neighbor.

These indirect loves have a virtue that is exactly and rigorously equivalent. It depends on circumstances, temperament, and vocation which is the first to enter the soul; one or other of them is dominant during the period of preparation. It is not necessarily the same one for the whole of this period.

It is probable that in most cases the period of preparation does not draw toward its end, the soul is not ready to receive the personal visit of its Master, unless it has in it all three indirect loves to a high degree.

The combination of these loves constitutes the love of God in the form best suited to the preparatory period, that is to say a veiled form.

They do not disappear when the love of God in the full sense of the word wells up in the soul; they become infinitely stronger and all loves taken together make only a single love.

The veiled form of love necessarily comes first however and often reigns alone in the soul for a very long time. Perhaps, with a great many people, it may continue to do so till death. Veiled love can reach a very high degree of purity and power.

At the moment when it touches the soul, each of the forms that such love may take has the virtue of a sacrament.

THE LOVE OF OUR NEIGHBOR

Christ made this clear enough with regard to the love of our neighbor. He said that he would one day thank his benefactors, saying to them: "I was anhungered and ye gave me meat." Who but Christ himself can be Christ's benefactor? How can a man give meat to Christ, if he is not raised at least for a moment to the state spoken of by Saint Paul, when he no longer lives in himself but Christ lives in him?

The text of the Gospel is concerned only with Christ's presence in the sufferer. Yet it seems as though the spiritual worthiness of him who receives has nothing to do with the matter. It must then be admitted that it is the benefactor himself, as a bearer of Christ, who causes Christ to enter the famished sufferer with the bread he gives him. The other can consent to receive this presence or not, exactly like the person who goes to communion. If the gift is rightly given and rightly received, the passing of a morsel of bread from one man to another is something like a real communion.

Christ does not call his benefactors loving or charitable. He calls them just. The Gospel makes no distinction between the love of our neighbor and justice. In the eyes of the Greeks also a respect for Zeus the suppliant was the first duty of justice. We have invented the distinction between justice and charity. It is easy to understand why. Our notion of justice dispenses him who possesses from the obligation of giving. If he gives all the same, he thinks he has a right to be pleased with himself. He thinks he has done a good work. As for him who receives, it depends on the way he interprets this notion whether he is exempted from all gratitude or whether it obliges him to offer servile thanks.

Only the absolute identification of justice and love makes the coexistence possible of compassion and gratitude on the one hand, and on the other, of respect for the dignity of affliction in the afflicted—a respect felt by the sufferer himself and the others.

It has to be recognized that no kindness can go further than justice without constituting a fault under a false appearance of kindness. But the just must be thanked for being just, because justice is so beautiful a thing, in the same way as we thank God because of his great glory. Any other gratitude is servile and even animal.

The only difference between the man who witnesses an act of justice and the man who receives a material advantage from it is that in such circumstances the beauty of justice is only a spectacle for the first, while for the second it is the object of a contact and even a kind of nourishment. Thus the feeling which is simple admiration in the first should be carried to a far higher degree in the second by the fire of gratitude.

To be ungrateful when we have been treated with justice, in circumstances where injustice is easily possible, is to deprive ourselves of the supernatural and sacramental virtue contained in every pure act of justice.

Nothing better enables us to form a conception of this virtue than the doctrine of natural justice as we find it set forth with an incomparable integrity of spirit in a few marvelous lines of Thucydides.

The Athenians, who were at war with Sparta, wanted to force the inhabitants of the little island of Melos, allied to Sparta from all antiquity and so far remaining neutral, to join with them. It was in vain that the men of Melos, faced with the ultimatum of the Athenians, invoked justice, imploring pity for the antiquity of their town. As they would not give in, the Athenians razed their city to the ground, put all their men to death, and sold all their women and children as slaves.

Thucydides has put the lines in question into the mouth of these Athenians. They begin by saying that they will not try to prove that their ultimatum is just.

"Let us treat rather of what is possible.... You know it as well as we do; the human spirit is so constituted that what is just is only examined if there is equal necessity on both sides. But if one is strong and the other weak, that which is possible is imposed by the first and accepted by the second."

The men of Melos said that in the case of a battle they would have the gods with them on account of the justice of their cause. The Athenians replied that they saw no reason to suppose so.

"As touching the gods we have the belief, and as touching men the certainty, that always, by a necessity of nature, each one commands wherever he has the power. We did not establish this law, we are not the first to apply it; we found it already established, we abide by it as something likely to endure forever; and that is why we apply it. We know quite well that you also, like all the others, once you reached the same degree of power, would act in the same way."

Such lucidity of mind in the conception of injustice is the

light that comes immediately below that of charity. It is the clarity that sometimes remains where charity once existed but has become extinguished. Below comes the darkness in which the strong sincerely believe that their cause is more just than that of the weak. That was the case with the Romans and the Hebrews.

Possibility and necessity are terms opposed to justice in these lines. Possible means all that the strong can impose upon the weak. It is reasonable to examine how far this possibility goes. Supposing it to be known, it is certain that the strong will accomplish his purpose to the extreme limit of possibility. It is a mechanical necessity. Otherwise it would be as though he willed and did not will simultaneously. There is a necessity for the strong as well as the weak in this.

When two human beings have to settle something and neither has the power to impose anything on the other, they have to come to an understanding. Then justice is consulted, for justice alone has the power to make two wills coincide. It is the image of that Love which in God unites the Father and Son, and which is the common thought of separate thinkers. But when there is a strong and a weak there is no need to unite their wills. There is only one will, that of the strong. The weak obeys. Everything happens just as it does when a man is handling matter. There are not two wills to be made to coincide. The man wills and the matter submits. The weak are like things. There is no difference between throwing a stone to get rid of a troublesome dog and saying to a slave: "Chase that dog away."

Beyond a certain degree of inequality in the relations of

men of unequal strength, the weaker passes into the state of matter and loses his personality. The men of old used to say: "A man loses half his soul the day he becomes a slave."

The even balance, an image of equal relations of strength, was the symbol of justice from all antiquity, specially in Egypt. It may have had a religious purpose before being used for commerce. Its use in trade is the image of the mutual consent, the very essence of justice, which should be the rule in exchanges. The definition of justice as being made up of mutual consent, which is found in the legislation of Sparta, probably originated in the Aegeo-Cretan civilization.

The supernatural virtue of justice consists of behaving exactly as though there were equality when one is the stronger in an unequal relationship. Exactly, in every respect, including the slightest details of accent and attitude, for a detail may be enough to place the weaker party in the condition of matter, which on this occasion naturally belongs to him, just as the slightest shock causes water that has remained liquid below freezing point to solidify.

Supernatural virtue, for the inferior thus treated, consists in not believing that there really is equality of strength and in recognizing that his treatment is due solely to the generosity of the other party. That is what is called gratitude. For the inferior treated in a different way, the supernatural virtue of justice consists in understanding that the treatment he is undergoing, though on the one hand differing from justice, on the other is in conformity with necessity and the mechanism of human nature. He should avoid both submission and revolt.

He who treats as equals those who are far below him in strength really makes them a gift of the quality of human beings, of which fate had deprived them. As far as it is possible for a creature, he reproduces the original generosity of the Creator with regard to them.

This is the most Christian of virtues. It is also the virtue that the Egyptian *Book of the Dead* describes in words as sublime even as those of the Gospel. "I have never caused anyone to weep. I have never spoken with a haughty voice. I have never made anyone afraid. I have never been deaf to words of justice and truth."

Gratitude on the part of the unfortunate, when it is pure, is but a participation in this same virtue, for only he who is capable of it can recognize it. Others experience the results of it without any recognition.

Such virtue is identical with real, active faith in the true God. The Athenians of Thucydides thought that divinity, like humanity in its natural state, always carried its power of commanding to the extreme limit of possibility.

The true God is the God we think of as almighty, but as not exercising his power everywhere, for he is found only in the heavens or in secret here below.

Those of the Athenians who massacred the inhabitants of Melos had no longer any idea of such a God.

The first proof that they were in the wrong lies in the fact that, contrary to their assertion, it happens, although extremely rarely, that a man will forbear out of pure generosity to command where he has the power to do so. That which is possible for man is possible also for God.

The examples of this may be challenged, but it is certain that if in one or another example it can be proved that the sole motive is pure generosity, such generosity will be generally admired. All that man is capable of admiring is possible with God.

The spectacle of this world is another, more certain proof. Pure goodness is not anywhere to be found in it. Either God is not almighty or he is not absolutely good, or else he does not command everywhere where he has the power to do so.

Thus the existence of evil here below, far from disproving the reality of God, is the very thing that reveals him in his truth.

On God's part creation is not an act of self-expansion but of restraint and renunciation. God and all his creatures are less than God alone. God accepted this diminution. He emptied a part of his being from himself. He had already emptied himself in this act of his divinity; that is why Saint John says that the Lamb had been slain from the beginning of the world. God permitted the existence of things distinct from himself and worth infinitely less than himself. By this creative act he denied himself, as Christ has told us to deny ourselves. God denied himself for our sakes in order to give us the possibility of denying ourselves for him. This response, this echo, which it is in our power to refuse, is the only possible justification for the folly of love of the creative act.

The religions which have a conception of this renunciation, this voluntary distance, this voluntary effacement of God, his apparent absence and his secret presence here below, these religions are true religion, the translation into different languages of the great Revelation. The religions which represent divinity as commanding wherever it has the power to do so seem false. Even though they are monotheistic they are idolatrous.

He who, being reduced by affliction to the state of an inert and passive thing, returns, at least for a time, to the state of a human being, through the generosity of others; such a one, if he knows how to accept and feel the true essence of this generosity, receives at the very instant a soul begotten exclusively of charity. He is born from on high of water and of the Spirit. (The word in the Gospel, *anōthen*, means from on high more often than again.) To treat our neighbor who is in affliction with love is something like baptizing him.

He from whom the act of generosity proceeds can only behave as he does if his thought transports him into the other. At such a moment he also consists only of water and of the Spirit.

Generosity and compassion are inseparable, and both have their model in God, that is to say, in creation and in the Passion.

Christ taught us that the supernatural love of our neighbor is the exchange of compassion and gratitude which happens in a flash between two beings, one possessing and the other deprived of human personality. One of the two is only a little piece of flesh, naked, inert, and bleeding beside a ditch; he is nameless; no one knows anything about him. Those who pass by this thing scarcely notice it, and a few minutes afterward do not even know that they saw it. Only

The neighbor is the afflicted.

one stops and turns his attention toward it. The actions that follow are just the automatic effect of this moment of attention. The attention is creative. But at the moment when it is engaged it is a renunciation. This is true, at least, if it is pure. The man accepts to be diminished by concentrating on an expenditure of energy, which will not extend his own power but will only give existence to a being other than himself, who will exist independently of him. Still more, to desire the existence of the other is to transport himself into him by sympathy, and, as a result, to have a share in the state of inert matter which is his.

Such an operation goes equally against the nature of a man who has not known affliction and is ignorant of its meaning, and a man who has known or had a foretaste of affliction and whom it fills with horror.

It is not surprising that a man who has bread should give a piece to someone who is starving. What is surprising is that he should be capable of doing so with so different a gesture from that with which we buy an object. Almsgiving when it is not supernatural is like a sort of purchase. It buys the sufferer.

Whatever a man may want, in cases of crime as in those of the highest virtue, in the minutest preoccupations as in the greatest designs, the essence of his desire always consists in this, that he wants above all things to be able to exercise his will freely. To wish for the existence of this free consent in another, deprived of it by affliction, is to transport oneself into him; it is to consent to affliction oneself, that is to say to the destruction of oneself. It is to deny oneself. In denying oneself, one becomes capable under God of establishing someone else by a creative affirmation. One gives oneself in ransom for the other. It is a redemptive act.

The sympathy of the weak for the strong is natural, for the weak in putting himself into the place of the other acquires an imaginary strength. The sympathy of the strong for the weak, being in the opposite direction, is against nature.

That is why the sympathy of the weak for the strong is pure only if its sole object is the sympathy received from the other, when the other is truly generous. This is super-natural gratitude, which means gladness to be the recipient of supernatural compassion. It leaves self-respect absolutely intact. The preservation of true self-respect in affliction is also something supernatural. Gratitude that is pure, like pure compassion, is essentially the acceptance of affliction. The afflicted man and his benefactor, between whom diversity of fortune places an infinite distance, are united in this acceptance. There is friendship between them in the sense of the Pythagoreans, miraculous harmony and equality.

Both of them recognize at the same time, with all their soul, that it is better not to command wherever one has power to do so. If this thought fills the whole soul and controls the imagination, which is the source of our actions, it constitutes true faith. For it places the Good outside this world, where are all the sources of power; it recognizes it as the archetype of the secret point that lies at the center of human personality and is the principle of renunciation.

Even in art and science, though second-class work, brilliant or mediocre, is an extension of the self; work of the very highest order, true creation, means self-loss. We do not perceive this truth, because fame confuses and covers with its glory achievements of the highest order and the most brilliant productions of the second class, often giving the advantage to the latter.

Love for our neighbor, being made of creative attention, is analogous to genius.

Creative attention means really giving our attention to what does not exist. Humanity does not exist in the anonymous flesh lying inert by the roadside. The Samaritan who stops and looks gives his attention all the same to this absent humanity, and the actions which follow prove that it is a question of real attention.

"Faith," says Saint Paul, "is the evidence of things not seen." * In this moment of attention faith is present as much as love.

In the same way a man who is entirely at the disposal of others does not exist. A slave does not exist either in the eyes of his master or in his own. When the Negro slaves in America accidentally hurt their feet or their hands, they used to say: "It does not matter, it is the master's foot, the master's hand." He who has absolutely no belongings of any kind around which social consideration crystallizes does not exist. A popular Spanish song says in words of marvelous truth: "If anyone wants to make himself invisible, there is no surer way than to become poor." Love sees what is invisible.

God *thought* that which did not exist, and by this thought brought it into being. At each moment we exist only because God consents to think us into being, although really

* Hebrews 11:1.

149

we have no existence. At any rate that is how we represent creation to ourselves, humanly and hence inadequately of course, but this imagery contains an element of truth. God alone has this power, the power really to think into being that which does not exist. Only God, present in us, can really think the human quality into the victims of affliction, can really look at them with a look differing from that we give to things, can listen to their voice as we listen to spoken words. Then they become aware that they have a voice, otherwise they would not have occasion to notice it.

Difficult as it is really to listen to someone in affliction, it is just as difficult for him to know that compassion is listening to him.

The love of our neighbor is the love which comes down from God to man. It precedes that which rises from men to God. God is longing to come down to those in affliction. As soon as a soul is disposed to consent, though it were the last, the most miserable, the most deformed of souls, God will precipitate himself into it in order, through it, to look at and listen to the afflicted. Only as time passes does the soul become aware that he is there. But, though it finds no name for him, wherever the afflicted are loved for themselves alone, it is God who is present.

God is not present, even if we invoke him, where the afflicted are merely regarded as an occasion for doing good. They may even be loved on this account, but then they are in their natural role, the role of matter and of things. We have to bring to them in their inert, anonymous condition a personal love.

That is why expressions such as to love our neighbor in God, or for God, are misleading and equivocal. A man has all he can do, even if he concentrates all the attention of which he is capable, to look at this small inert thing of flesh, lying stripped of clothing by the roadside. It is not the time to turn his thoughts toward God. Just as there are times when we must think of God and forget all creatures without exception, there are times when, as we look at creatures, we do not have to think explicitly of God. At such times, the presence of God in us has as its condition a secret so deep that it is even a secret from us. There are times when thinking of God separates us from him. Modesty is the condition of nuptial union.

In true love it is not we who love the afflicted in God; it is God in us who loves them. When we are in affliction, it is God in us who loves those who wish us well. Compassion and gratitude come down from God, and when they are exchanged in a glance, God is present at the point where the eyes of those who give and those who receive meet. The sufferer and the other love each other, starting from God, through God, but not for the love of God; they love each other for the love of the one for the other. This is an impossibility. That is why it comes about only through the agency of God.

He who gives bread to the famished sufferer for the love of God will not be thanked by Christ. He has already had his reward in this thought itself. Christ thanks those who do not know to whom they are giving food.

Moreover, giving is only one of the two possible forms love for the afflicted may take. Power always means power to do good or to hurt. In a relationship where the strength is very unequally divided, the superior can be just toward the inferior either in doing him good with justice or in hurting him with justice. In the first case we have almsgiving; in the second, punishment.

Just punishment, like just almsgiving, enshrines the real presence of God and constitutes something in the nature of a sacrament. That also is made quite clear in the Gospel. It is expressed by the words: "He that is without sin among you let him first cast a stone." Christ alone is without sin.

Christ spared the woman taken in adultery. The administration of punishment was not in accordance with the earthly life which was to end on the Cross. He did not however prescribe the abolition of penal justice. He allowed stoning to continue. Wherever it is done with justice, it is therefore he who throws the first stone. As he dwells in the famished wretch whom a just man feeds, so he dwells in the condemned wretch whom a just man punishes. He did not say so, but he showed it clearly enough by dying like a common criminal. He is the divine model of prisoners and old offenders. As the young workingmen of the J.O.C.* thrill at the thought that Christ is one of them, so condemned criminals have just reason to taste a like rapture. They only need to be told, as the working men were told. In a sense Christ is nearer to them than to the martyrs.

The stone which slays and the piece of bread which provides nourishment have exactly the same virtue if Christ is present at the start and the finish. The gift of life and the gift of death are equivalent.

* *Jeunesse Ouvrière Catholique*, cf. note on *Jécistes*.

According to the Hindu tradition, King Rama, the incarnation of the Second Person of the Trinity, was obliged, much to his regret, to avoid scandal among his people by executing a man of low caste who had broken the law through giving himself up to the ascetic practice of religion. The King went himself to find the man and slew him with a stroke of his sword. Immediately afterward the soul of the dead man appeared to him and fell at his feet, thanking him for the degree of glory conferred upon him by the contact of this blessed sword. Thus the execution, although quite unjust in one sense, but legal and carried out by the very hand of God, had had in it all the virtue of a sacrament.

The legal character of a punishment has no true significance if it does not give it some kind of religious meaning, if it does not make of it the analogy of a sacrament; and therefore all penal offices, from that of the judge to that of the executioner and the prison guard, should in some sort share in the priestly office.

Justice in punishment can be defined in the same way as justice in almsgiving. It means giving our attention to the victim of affliction as to a being and not a thing; it means wishing to preserve in him the faculty of free consent.

Men think they are despising crime when they are really despising the weakness of affliction. A being in whom the two are combined affords them an opportunity of giving free play to their contempt for affliction on the pretext that they are scorning crime. He is thus the object of the greatest contempt. Contempt is the contrary of attention. There are exceptions only where there is a crime which for some reason has prestige, as is often the case with murder on account of the fleeting moment of power which it implies, or where the crime does not make a very vivid impression upon those who assess its culpability. Stealing is the crime most devoid of prestige, and it causes most indignation because property is the thing to which people are most generally and powerfully attached. That is apparent even in the penal code.

No state is beneath that of a human being enveloped in a cloud of guilt, be it true or false, and entirely in the power of a few men who are to decide his fate with a word. These men do not pay any attention to him. Moreover, from the moment when anyone falls into the hands of the law with all its penal machinery until the moment he is free again—and those known as hardened criminals are like prostitutes, in that they hardly ever do get free until the day of their death—such a one is never an object of attention. Everything combines, down to the smallest details, down even to the inflections of people's voices, to make him seem vile and outcast in all men's eyes including his own. The brutality and flippancy, the terms of scorn and the jokes, the way of speaking, the way of listening and of not listening, all these things are equally effective.

There is no intentional unkindness in it all. It is the automatic effect of a professional life which has as its object crime seen in the form of affliction, that is to say in the form where horror and defilement are exposed in their nakedness. Such a contact, being uninterrupted, necessarily contaminates, and the form this contamination takes is contempt. It is this contempt which is reflected on every prisoner at the bar. The penal apparatus is like a transmitter which turns the whole volume of defilement contained in all the circles where the miserable crime is to be found upon each accused person. The mere contact with this penal apparatus causes a kind of horror in that part of the soul remaining intact, and the horror is in exact proportion to the innocence. Those who are completely rotten receive no injury and do not suffer.

It cannot be otherwise, if there is not something between the penal apparatus and the crime capable of cleansing defilement. This can only be God. Infinite purity alone is not contaminated by contact with evil. All finite purity becomes defilement itself through prolonged contact. However the code may be reformed, punishment cannot be humane unless it passes through Christ.

The severity of the sentence is not the most important thing. Under present conditions, a condemned man, although guilty and given a punishment which is relatively light in view of his offense, can more often than not be rightly considered as having been the victim of a cruel injustice. What is important is that the punishment should be legitimate, that is to say that it should proceed directly from the law. It is important that the law should be recognized as having a divine character, not because of its content but because it is law. It is important that the whole organization of penal justice should be directed toward obtaining from the magistrates and their assistants the attention and respect for the accused that is due from every man to any person who may be in his power and from the accused his consent to the punishment inflicted, a consent of which the innocent Christ has given us the perfect model.

A death sentence for a slight offense, pronounced in such a way, would be less horrible than a sentence of six months in prison given as it is at the present day. Nothing is more frightful than the spectacle, now so frequent, of an accused, whose situation provides him with nothing to fall back upon but his own words, and who is incapable of arranging these words because of his social origin and lack of culture, as he stands broken down by guilt, affliction, and fear, stammering before judges who are not listening and who interrupt him in tones of ostentatious refinement.

For as long as affliction is to be found in society, for as long as legal or private almsgiving and punishment are inevitable, the separation between civil institutions and religious life will be a crime. The lay conception considered alone is completely false. It only has some excuse as a reaction against a totalitarian religion. In that respect, it must be admitted, it is partly justifiable.

In order to be present everywhere, as it should, religion must not only not be totalitarian, but it must limit itself strictly to the plane of supernatural love which alone is suitable for it. If it did so it would penetrate everywhere. The Bible says: "Wisdom penetrates everywhere on account of its perfect purity."

Through the absence of Christ, mendicity, in the widest sense of the word, and penal action are perhaps the most frightful things on earth—two things that are almost infernal. They have the very color of hell. Prostitution might be added to them, for it is to real marriage what almsgiving and punishment without charity are to almsgiving and punishment which are just.

Men have received the power to do good or harm not only to the body but to the souls of their fellows, to the whole soul of those in whom God is not present and to all that part of the soul uninhabited by God of the others. A man may be indwelt by God, by the power of evil or merely by the mechanism of the flesh. When he gives or punishes, what he bears within him enters the soul of the other through the bread or the sword. The substance of the bread and the sword are virgin, empty of good and of evil, equally capable of conveying one or the other. He who is forced by affliction to receive bread or to suffer chastisement has his soul exposed naked and defenseless both to evil and to good.

There is only one way of never receiving anything but good. It is to know, with our whole soul and not just abstractly, that men who are not animated by pure charity are merely wheels in the mechanism of the order of the world, like inert matter. After that we see that everything comes directly from God, either through the love of a man, or through the lifelessness of matter, whether it be tangible or psychic; through spirit or water. All that increases the vital energy in us is like the bread for which Christ thanks the just. All the blows, the wounds, and the mutilations are like a stone thrown at us by the hand of Christ. Bread and stone both come from Christ and penetrating to our inward being bring Christ into us. Bread and stone are love. We must eat the bread and lay ourselves open to the stone, so that it may sink as deeply as possible into our flesh. If we have any armor able to protect our soul from the stones thrown by Christ, we should take it off and cast it away.

LOVE OF THE ORDER OF THE WORLD

The love of the order and beauty of the world is thus the complement of the love of our neighbor.

It proceeds from the same renunciation, the renunciation that is an image of the creative renunciation of God. God causes this universe to exist, but he consents not to command it, although he has the power to do so. Instead he leaves two other forces to rule in his place. On the one hand there is the blind necessity attaching to matter, including the psychic matter of the soul, and on the other the autonomy essential to thinking persons.

By loving our neighbor we imitate the divine love which created us and all our fellows. By loving the order of the world we imitate the divine love which created this universe of which we are a part.

Man does not have to renounce the command of matter and of souls, since he does not possess the power to command them. But God has conferred upon him an imaginary likeness of this power, an imaginary divinity, so that he also, although a creature, may empty himself of his divinity.

Just as God, being outside the universe, is at the same time the center, so each man imagines he is situated in the center of the world. The illusion of perspective places him at the center of space; an illusion of the same kind falsifies his idea of time; and yet another kindred illusion arranges a whole hierarchy of values around him. This illusion is extended even to our sense of existence, on account of the intimate connection between our sense of value and our sense of being; being seems to us less and less concentrated the farther it is removed from us.

We relegate the spatial form of this illusion to the place where it belongs, the realm of the imagination. We are obliged to do so; otherwise we should not perceive a single object; we should not even be able to direct ourselves enough to take a single step consciously. God thus provides us with a model of the operation which should transform all our soul. In the same way as in our infancy we learn to control and check this illusion in our sense of space, we should control and check it in our sense of time, values, and being. Otherwise from every point of view except that of space we shall be incapable of discerning a single object or directing a single step.

We live in a world of unreality and dreams. To give up our imaginary position as the center, to renounce it, not only intellectually but in the imaginative part of our soul, that means to awaken to what is real and eternal, to see the true light and hear the true silence. A transformation then takes place at the very roots of our sensibility, in our immediate reception of sense impressions and psychological impressions. It is a transformation analogous to that which takes place in the dusk of evening on a road, where we suddenly discern as a tree what we had at first seen as a stooping man; or where we suddenly recognize as a rustling of leaves what we thought at first was whispering voices. We see the same colors; we hear the same sounds, but not in the same way.

To empty ourselves of our false divinity, to deny ourselves, to give up being the center of the world in imagina-

[Handwritten margin notes: The only free choice is to choose to believe our illusionary this... state. And this realization is only... reducing freedom to... illusion and illusion... that does nothing except to accept... qualities of world as... unchangeable.]

tion, to discern that all points in the world are equally centers and that the true center is outside the world, this is to consent to the rule of mechanical necessity in matter and of free choice at the center of each soul. Such consent is love. The face of this love, which is turned toward thinking persons, is the love of our neighbor; the face turned toward matter is love of the order of the world, or love of the beauty of the world which is the same thing.

In ancient times the love of the beauty of the world had a very important place in men's thoughts and surrounded the whole of life with marvelous poetry. This was the case in every nation—in China, in India, and in Greece. The Stoicism of the Greeks, which was very wonderful and to which primitive Christianity was infinitely close, especially in the writings of Saint John, was almost exclusively the love of the beauty of the world. As for Israel, certain parts of the Old Testament, the Psalms, the Book of Job, Isaiah, and the Book of Wisdom, contain an incomparable expression of the beauty of the world.

The example of Saint Francis shows how great a place the beauty of the world can have in Christian thought. Not only is his actual poem perfect poetry, but all his life was perfect poetry in action. His very choice of places for solitary retreats or for the foundations of his convents was in itself the most beautiful poetry in action. Vagabondage and poverty were poetry with him; he stripped himself naked in order to have immediate contact with the beauty of the world.

Saint John of the Cross also has some beautiful lines about the beauty of the world. But in general, making suitable reservations for the treasures that are unknown, little known, or perhaps buried among the forgotten remains of the Middle Ages, we might say that the beauty of the world is almost absent from the Christian tradition. This is strange. It is difficult to understand. It leaves a terrible gap. How can Christianity call itself catholic if the universe itself is left out?

It is true that there is little mention of the beauty of the world in the Gospel. But in so short a text, which, as Saint John says, is very far from containing all that Christ taught, the disciples no doubt thought it unnecessary to put anything so generally accepted.

It does, however, come up on two occasions. Once Christ tells us to contemplate and imitate the lilies of the field and the birds of the air, in their indifference as to the future and their docile acceptance of destiny; and another time he invites us to contemplate and imitate the indiscriminate distribution of rain and sunlight.

The Renaissance thought to renew its spiritual links with antiquity by passing over Christianity, but it hardly took anything but the secondary products of ancient civilization —art, science, and curiosity regarding human things. It scarcely touched the fringe of the central inspiration. It failed to rediscover any link with the beauty of the world.

In the eleventh and twelfth centuries there had been the beginning of a Renaissance which would have been the real one if it had been able to bear fruit; it began to germinate notably in Languedoc. Some of the Troubadour poems on spring lead one to think that perhaps Christian inspiration and the beauty of the world would not have been separated had it developed. Moreover the spirit of Languedoc left its mark on Italy and was perhaps not unrelated to the Franciscan inspiration. But, whether it be coincidence or more probably the connection of cause and effect, these germs did not survive the war of the Albigenses and only traces of the movement were found after that.

Today one might think that the white races had almost lost all feeling for the beauty of the world, and that they had taken upon them the task of making it disappear from all the continents where they have penetrated with their armies, their trade and their religion. As Christ said to the Pharisees: "Woe to you, for ye have taken away the key of knowledge; ye entered not in yourselves and them that were entering in ye hindered." *

And yet at the present time, in the countries of the white races, the beauty of the world is almost the only way by which we can allow God to penetrate us, for we are still farther removed from the other two. Real love and respect for religious practices are rare even among those who are most assiduous in observing them, and are practically never to be found in others. Most people do not even conceive them to be possible. As regards the supernatural purpose of affliction, compassion and gratitude are not only rare but have become almost unintelligible for almost everyone today. The very idea of them has almost disappeared; the very meaning of the words has been debased.

On the other hand a sense of beauty, although mutilated, distorted, and soiled, remains rooted in the heart of man as a powerful incentive. It is present in all the preoccupations

* Luke 11:52.

162

of secular life. If it were made true and pure, it would sweep all secular life in a body to the feet of God; it would make the total incarnation of the faith possible.

Moreover, speaking generally, the beauty of the world is the commonest, easiest, and most natural way of approach.

Just as God hastens into every soul immediately it opens, even a little, in order through it to love and serve the afflicted, so he descends in all haste to love and admire the tangible beauty of his own creation through the soul that opens to him.

But the contrary is still more true. The soul's natural inclination to love beauty is the trap God most frequently uses in order to win it and open it to the breath from on high.

This was the trap which enticed Cora. All the heavens above were smiling at the scent of the narcissus; so was the entire earth and all the swelling ocean. Hardly had the poor girl stretched out her hand before she was caught in the trap. She fell into the hands of the living God. When she escaped she had eaten the seed of the pomegranate which bound her for ever. She was no longer a virgin; she was the spouse of God.

The beauty of the world is the mouth of a labyrinth. The unwary individual who on entering takes a few steps is soon unable to find the opening. Worn out, with nothing to eat or drink, in the dark, separated from his dear ones, and from everything he loves and is accustomed to, he walks on without knowing anything or hoping anything, incapable even of discovering whether he is really going forward or merely turning round on the same spot. But this affliction is as nothing compared with the danger threatening him. For if he does not lose courage, if he goes on walking, it is absolutely certain that he will finally arrive at the center of the labyrinth. And there God is waiting to eat him. Later he will go out again, but he will be changed, he will have become different, after being eaten and digested by God. Afterward he will stay near the entrance so that he can gently push all those who come near into the opening.

The beauty of the world is not an attribute of matter in itself. It is a relationship of the world to our sensibility, the sensibility that depends upon the structure of our body and our soul. The Micromegas of Voltaire, a thinking infusorian organism, could have had no access to the beauty on which we live in the universe. We must have faith that, supposing such creatures were to exist, the world would be beautiful for them too; but it would be beautiful in another way. Anyhow we must have faith that the universe is beautiful on all levels, and more generally that it has a fullness of beauty in relation to the bodily and psychic structure of each of the thinking beings that actually do exist and of all those that are possible. It is this very agreement of an infinity of perfect beauties that gives a transcendent character to the beauty of the world. Nevertheless the part of this beauty we experience is designed and destined for our human sensibility.

The beauty of the world is the co-operation of divine wisdom in creation. "Zeus made all things," says an Orphic line, "and Bacchus perfected them." This perfecting is the creation of beauty; God created the universe, and his Son, our first-born brother, created the beauty of it for us. The beauty of the world is Christ's tender smile for us coming through matter. He is really present in the universal beauty. The love of this beauty proceeds from God dwelling in our souls and goes out to God present in the universe. It also is like a sacrament.

This is true only of universal beauty. With the exception of God, nothing short of the universe as a whole can with complete accuracy be called beautiful. All that is in the universe and is less than the universe can be called beautiful only if we extend the word beyond its strict limits and apply it to things that share indirectly in beauty, things that are imitations of it.

All these secondary kinds of beauty are of infinite value as openings to universal beauty. But, if we stop short at them, they are, on the contrary, veils; then they corrupt. They all have in them more or less of this temptation, but in very different degrees.

There are also a number of seductive factors which have nothing whatever to do with beauty but which cause the things in which they are present to be called beautiful through lack of discernment; for these things attract love by fraud, and all men, even the most ignorant, even the vilest of them, know that beauty alone has a right to our love. The most truly great know it too. No man is below or above beauty. The words which express beauty come to the lips of all as soon as they want to praise what they love. Only some are more and some less able to discern it.

Beauty is the only finality here below. As Kant said very aptly, it is a finality which involves no objective. A beautiful thing involves no good except itself, in its totality, as it

165

appears to us. We are drawn toward it without knowing what to ask of it. It offers us its own existence. We do not desire anything else, we possess it, and yet we still desire something. We do not in the least know what it is. We want to get behind beauty, but it is only a surface. It is like a mirror that sends us back our own desire for goodness. It is a sphinx, an enigma, a mystery which is painfully tantalizing. We should like to feed upon it but it is merely something to look at; it appears only from a certain distance. The great trouble in human life is that looking and eating are two different operations. Only beyond the sky, in the country inhabited by God, are they one and the same operation. Children feel this trouble already, when they look at a cake for a long time almost regretting that it should have to be eaten and yet are unable to help eating it. It may be that vice, depravity, and crime are nearly always, or even perhaps always, in their essence, attempts to eat beauty, to eat what we should only look at. Eve began it. If she caused humanity to be lost by eating the fruit, the opposite attitude, looking at the fruit without eating it, should be what is required to save it. "Two winged companions," says an Upanishad, "two birds are on the branch of a tree. One eats the fruit, the other looks at it." These two birds are the two parts of our soul.

It is because beauty has no end in view that it constitutes the only finality here below. For here below there are no ends. All the things that we take for ends are means. That is an obvious truth. Money is the means of buying, power is the means of commanding. It is more or less the same for all the things that we call good.

Only beauty is not the means to anything else. It alone is good in itself, but without our finding any particular good or advantage in it. It seems itself to be a promise and not a good. But it only gives itself; it never gives anything else.

Nevertheless, as it is the only finality, it is present in all human pursuits. Although they are all concerned with means, for everything that exists here below is only a means, beauty sheds a luster upon them which colors them with finality. Otherwise there could neither be desire, nor, in consequence, energy in the pursuit.

For a miser after the style of Harpagon, all the beauty of the world is enshrined in gold. And it is true that gold, as a pure and shining substance, has something beautiful about it. The disappearance of gold from our currency seems to have made this form of avarice disappear too. Today those who heap up money without spending it are desirous of power.

Most of those who seek riches connect the thought of luxury with them. Luxury is the finality of riches. Moreover luxury itself represents beauty for a whole class of men. It provides surroundings through which they can feel in a vague fashion that the universe is beautiful; just as Saint Francis needed to be a vagabond and a beggar in order to feel it to be beautiful. Either way would be equally legitimate if in each case the beauty of the world were experienced in an equally direct, pure, and full manner; but happily God willed that it should not be so. Poverty has a privilege. That is a dispensation of Providence without which the love of the beauty of the world might easily come into conflict with the love of our neighbor. Nevertheless, the horror of poverty—and every reduction of wealth can be felt as poverty, even its failure to increase—is essentially a horror of ugliness. The soul that is prevented by circumstances from feeling anything of the beauty of the world, even confusedly, even through what is false, is invaded to its very center by a kind of horror.

The love of power amounts to a desire to establish order among the men and things around oneself, either on a large or small scale, and this desire for order is the result of a sense of beauty. In this case, as in the case of luxury, the question is one of forcing a certain circle into a pattern suggestive of universal beauty; this circle is limited, but the hope of increasing it indefinitely may often be present. This unsatisfied appetite, the desire to keep on increasing, is due precisely to a desire for contact with universal beauty, even though the circle we are organizing is not the universe. It is not the universe and it hides it. Our immediate universe is like the scenery in a theater.

In his poem *Sémiramis*, Valéry succeeds very well in making us feel the connection between tyranny and the love of beauty. Apart from war, the instrument for increasing his power, Louis XIV was only interested in festivals and architecture. Moreover war itself, especially as conducted in the old days, stirs man's sense of beauty in a way that is vital and poignant.

Art is an attempt to transport into a limited quantity of matter, modeled by man, an image of the infinite beauty of the entire universe. If the attempt succeeds, this portion of matter should not hide the universe, but on the contrary it should reveal its reality to all around.

Works of art that are neither pure and true reflections of the beauty of the world nor openings onto this beauty are not strictly speaking beautiful; their authors may be very talented but they lack real genius. That is true of a great many works of art which are among the most celebrated and the most highly praised. Every true artist has had real, direct, and immediate contact with the beauty of the world, contact that is of the nature of a sacrament. God has inspired every first-rate work of art, though its subject may be utterly and entirely secular; he has not inspired any of the others. Indeed the luster of beauty that distinguishes some of those others may quite well be a diabolical luster.

Science has as its object the study and the theoretical reconstruction of the order of the world—the order of the world in relation to the mental, psychic, and bodily structure of man. Contrary to the naïve illusions of certain scholars, neither the use of telescopes and microscopes, nor the employment of most unusual algebraical formulae, nor even a contempt for the principle of noncontradiction will allow it to get beyond the limits of this structure. Moreover it is not desirable that it should. The object of science is the presence of Wisdom in the universe, Wisdom of which we are the brothers, the presence of Christ, expressed through matter which constitutes the world.

We reconstruct for ourselves the order of the world in an image, starting from limited, countable, and strictly defined data. We work out a system for ourselves, establishing connections and conceiving of relationships between terms that are abstract and for that reason possible for us to deal with. Thus in an image, an image of which the very existence hangs upon an act of our attention, we can contemplate the necessity which is the substance of the universe but which, as such, only manifests itself to us by the blows it deals.

We cannot contemplate without a certain love. The contemplation of this image of the order of the world constitutes a certain contact with the beauty of the world. The beauty of the world is the order of the world that is loved.

Physical work is a specific contact with the beauty of the world, and can even be, in its best moments, a contact so full that no equivalent can be found elsewhere. The artist, the scholar, the philosopher, the contemplative should really admire the world and pierce through the film of unreality that veils it and makes of it, for nearly all men at nearly every moment of their lives, a dream or stage set. They ought to do this but more often than not they cannot manage it. He who is aching in every limb, worn out by the effort of a day of work, that is to say a day when he has been subject to matter, bears the reality of the universe in his flesh like a thorn. The difficulty for him is to look and to love. If he succeeds, he loves the Real.

That is the immense privilege God has reserved for his poor. But they scarcely ever know it. No one tells them. Excessive fatigue, harassing money worries, and the lack of true culture prevent them from noticing it. A slight change in these conditions would be enough to open the door to a treasure. It is heart-rending to see how easy it would be in many cases for men to procure a treasure for their fellows and how they allow centuries to pass without taking the trouble to do so.

At the time when there was a people's civilization, of which we are today collecting the crumbs as museum pieces under the name of folklore, the people doubtless had access to the treasure. Mythology too, which is very closely related to folklore, testifies to it, if we can decipher the poetry it contains.

Carnal love in all its forms, from the highest, that is to say true marriage or platonic love, down to the worst, down to debauchery, has the beauty of the world as its object. The love we feel for the splendor of the heavens, the plains, the sea, and the mountains, for the silence of nature which is borne in upon us by thousands of tiny sounds, for the breath of the winds or the warmth of the sun, this love of which every human being has at least an inkling, is an incomplete, painful love, because it is felt for things incapable of responding, that is to say for matter. Men want to turn this same love toward a being who is like themselves and capable of answering to their love, of saying yes, of surrendering. When the feeling for beauty happens to be associated with the sight of some human being, the transference of love is made possible, at any rate in an illusory manner. But it is all the beauty of the world, it is universal beauty, for which we yearn.

This kind of transference is what all love literature expresses, from the most ancient and well-worn metaphors and comparisons to the subtle analyses of Proust.

The longing to love the beauty of the world in a human being is essentially the longing for the Incarnation. It is mistaken if it thinks it is anything else. The Incarnation alone can satisfy it. It is therefore wrong to reproach the mystics, as has been done sometimes, because they use love's language. It is theirs by right. Others only borrow it.

If carnal Love on all levels goes more or less directly toward beauty—and the exceptions are perhaps only apparent—it is because beauty in a human being enables the imagination to see in him something like an equivalent of the order of the world.

That is why sins in this realm are serious. They constitute an offense against God from the very fact that the soul is unconsciously engaged in searching for God. Moreover they all come back to one thing and that is the more or less complete determination to dispense with consent. To be completely determined to dispense with it is perhaps the most frightful of all crimes. What can be more horrible than not to respect the consent of a being in whom one is seeking, though unconsciously, for an equivalent of God?

It is still a crime, though a less serious one, to be content with consent issuing from a low or superficial region of the soul. Whether there is physical union or not, the exchange of love is unlawful if, on both sides, the consent does not come from that central point in the soul where the yes can be nothing less than eternal. The obligation of marriage which is so often regarded as a simple social convention today, is implanted in the nature of human thought through the affinity between carnal love and beauty. Everything that is related to beauty should be unaffected by the passage of time. Beauty is eternity here below.

It is not surprising that in temptation men so often have the feeling of something absolute, which infinitely surpasses them, which they cannot resist. The absolute is indeed there. But we are mistaken when we think that it dwells in pleasure.

The mistake is the effect of this imaginary transference which is the principal mechanism of human thought. Job speaks of the slave who in death will cease to hear the voice of his master and who thinks that this voice harms him. It is but too true. The voice does him only too much harm. Yet he is mistaken. The voice is not harmful in itself. If he were not a slave it would not hurt him at all. But because he is a slave, the pain and the brutality of the blows of the whip enter his soul by the sense of hearing, at the same time as the voice, and penetrate to its very depths. There is no barrier by which he can protect himself. Affliction has forged this link.

In the same way the man who thinks he is in the power of pleasure is really in the power of the absolute which he has transferred to it. This absolute is to pleasure what the blows of the whip are to the master's voice; but the association is not the result of affliction here; it is the result of an original crime, the crime of idolatry. Saint Paul has emphasized the kinship between vice and idolatry.

He who has located the absolute in pleasure cannot help being dominated by it. Man does not struggle against the absolute. He who knows how to locate the absolute outside pleasure possesses the perfection of temperance.

The different kinds of vice, the use of drugs, in the literal or metaphorical sense of the word, all such things constitute the search for a state where the beauty of the world will be tangible. The mistake lies precisely in the search for a special state. False mysticism is another form of this error.

If the error is thrust deeply enough into the soul, man cannot but succumb to it.

In general all the tastes of men from the guiltiest to the most innocent, from the most usual to the most peculiar, are related to a combination of circumstances or to a set of people or surroundings which they imagine can give them access to the beauty of the world. The advantage of this or that group of circumstances is due to temperament, to the memories of a past life, to causes which are usually impossible to recognize.

There is only one case, which moreover is frequent, when the attraction of the pleasure of the senses does not lie in the contact it offers with beauty; it is when, on the contrary, it provides an escape from it.

The soul seeks nothing so much as contact with the beauty of the world, or at a still higher level, with God; but at the same time it flies from it. When the soul flies from anything it is always trying to get away, either from the horror of ugliness, or contact with what is truly pure. This is because all mediocrity flies from the light; and in all souls, except those which are near perfection, there is a great part which is mediocre. This part is seized with panic every time that a little pure beauty or pure goodness appears; it hides behind the flesh, it uses it as a veil. As a bellicose nation really needs to cover its aggression with some pretext or other if it is to succeed in its enterprises, the quality of the pretext being actually quite indifferent, so the mediocre part of the soul needs a slight pretext for flying from the light. The attraction of pleasure and the fear of pain supply this pretext. There again it is the absolute that dominates the soul, but as an object of repulsion and no longer as an at-traction. Very often also in the search for carnal pleasure the two movements are combined; the movement of run-ning toward pure beauty and the movement of flying far from it are indistinguishably tangled.

However it may be, in every kind of human occupation there is always some regard for the beauty of the world seen in more or less distorted or soiled images. As a consequence there is not any department of human life which is purely natural. The supernatural is secretly present throughout. Under a thousand different forms, grace and mortal sin are everywhere.

Between God and these incomplete, unconscious, often criminal searching for beauty, the only link is the beauty of the world. Christianity will not be incarnated so long as there is not joined to it the Stoic's idea of filial piety for the city of the world, for the country of here below which is the universe. When, as the result of some misapprehension, very difficult to understand today, Christianity cut itself off from Stoicism, it condemned itself to an abstract and sep-arate existence.

Even the very highest achievements of the search for beauty, in art or science for instance, are not truly beauti-ful. The only true beauty, the only beauty that is the real presence of God, is the beauty of the universe. Nothing less than the universe is beautiful.

The universe is beautiful as a beautiful work of art would be if there could be one that deserved this name. Thus it contains nothing constituting an end or a good in itself. It has in it no finality beyond universal beauty itself. The essential truth to be known concerning this universe is that it is absolutely devoid of finality. Nothing in the way of finality can be ascribed to it except through a lie or a mistake.

If we ask why such and such a word in a poem is in such and such a place and if there is an answer, either the poem is not of the highest order or else the reader has understood nothing of it. If one can rightly say that the word is where it is in order to express a particular idea, or for the sake of a grammatical connection, or for the sake of the rhyme or alliteration, or to complete the line, or to give a certain color, or even for a combination of several reasons of this kind, there has been a seeking for effect in the composition of the poem, there has not been true inspiration. In the case of a really beautiful poem the only answer is that the word is there because it is suitable that it should be. The proof of this suitability is that it is there and that the poem is beautiful. The poem is beautiful, that is to say the reader does not wish it other than it is.

It is in this way that art imitates the beauty of the world. The suitability of things, beings, and events consists only in this, that they exist and that we should not wish that they did not exist or that they had been different. Such a wish would be an impiety toward our universal country, a lack of the love of the Stoics. We are so constituted that this love is in fact possible; and it is this possibility of which the name is the beauty of the world.

The question of Beaumarchais: "Why these things rather than others?" never has any answer, because the world is devoid of finality. The absence of finality is the reign of

176

necessity. Things have causes and not ends. Those who think to discern special designs of Providence are like professors who give themselves up to what they call the explanation of the text, at the expense of a beautiful poem.

In art, the equivalent of this reign of necessity is the resistance of matter and arbitrary rules. Rhyme imposes upon the poet a direction in his choice of words which is absolutely unrelated to the sequence of ideas. Its function in poetry is perhaps analogous to that of affliction in our lives. Affliction forces us to feel with all our souls the absence of finality.

If the soul is set in the direction of love, the more we contemplate necessity, the more closely we press its metallic cold and hardness directly to our very flesh, the nearer we approach to the beauty of the world. That is what Job experienced. It was because he was so honest in his suffering, because he would not entertain any thought that might impair its truth, that God came down to reveal the beauty of the world to him.

It is because absence of any finality or intention is the essence of the beauty of the world that Christ told us to behold the rain and the light of the sun, as they fall without discrimination upon the just and the unjust. This recalls the supreme cry of Prometheus: "The heavens, where the common orb of day revolves for all." Christ commands us to imitate this beauty. Plato also in the Timæus counsels us through contemplation to make ourselves like to the beauty of the world, like to the harmony of the circular movements that cause day and night, months, seasons, and years to succeed each other and return. In these revolutions also, and in their combination, the absence of intention and finality is manifest; pure beauty shines forth.

It is because it can be loved by us, it is because it is beautiful, that the universe is a country. It is our only country here below. This thought is the essence of the wisdom of the Stoics. We have a heavenly country, but in a sense it is too difficult to love, because we do not know it; above all, in a sense, it is too easy to love, because we can imagine it as we please. We run the risk of loving a fiction under this name. If the love of the fiction is strong enough it makes all virtue easy, but at the same time of little value. Let us love the country of here below. It is real; it offers resistance to love. It is this country that God has given us to love. He has willed that it should be difficult yet possible to love it.

We feel ourselves to be outsiders, uprooted, in exile here below. We are like Ulysses who had been carried away during his sleep by sailors and woke in a strange land, longing for Ithaca with a longing that rent his soul. Suddenly Athena opened his eyes and he saw that he was in Ithaca. In the same way every man who longs indefatigably for his country, who is distracted from his desire neither by Calypso nor by the Sirens, will one day suddenly find that he is there.

The imitation of the beauty of the world, that which corresponds to the absence of finality, intention, and discrimination in it, is the absence of intention in ourselves, that is to say the renunciation of our own will. To be perfectly obedient is to be perfect as our Father in heaven is perfect.

Among men, a slave does not become like his master by

178

obeying him. On the contrary, the more he obeys the greater is the distance between them.

It is otherwise between man and God. If a reasonable creature is absolutely obedient, he becomes a perfect image of the Almighty as far as this is possible for him.

We are made in the very image of God. It is by virtue of something in us which attaches to the fact of being a person but which is not the fact itself. It is the power of renouncing our own personality. It is obedience.

Every time that a man rises to a degree of excellence, which by participation makes of him a divine being, we are aware of something impersonal and anonymous about him. His voice is enveloped in silence. This is evident in all the great works of art or thoughts, in the great deeds of saints and in their words.

It is then true in a sense that we must conceive of God as impersonal, in the sense that he is the divine model of a person who passes beyond the self by renunciation. To conceive of him as an all-powerful person, or under the name of Christ as a human person, is to exclude oneself from the true love of God. That is why we have to adore the perfection of the heavenly Father in his even diffusion of the light of the sun. The divine and absolute model of that renunciation which is obedience in us—such is the creative and ruling principle of the universe—such is the fullness of being.

It is because the renunciation of the personality makes man a reflection of God that it is so frightful to reduce men to the condition of inert matter by plunging them into affliction. When the quality of human personality is taken from them, the possibility of renouncing it is also taken away, except in the case of those who are sufficiently prepared. As God has created our independence so that we should have the possibility of renouncing it out of love, we should for the same reason wish to preserve the independence of our fellows. He who is perfectly obedient sets an infinite price upon the faculty of free choice in all men.

In the same way there is no contradiction between the love of the beauty of the world and compassion. Such love does not prevent us from suffering on our own account when we are in affliction. Neither does it prevent us from suffering because others are afflicted. It is on another plane from suffering.

The love of the beauty of the world, while it is universal, involves, as a love secondary and subordinate to itself, the love of all the truly precious things that bad fortune can destroy. The truly precious things are those forming ladders reaching toward the beauty of the world, openings onto it. He who has gone farther, to the very beauty of the world itself, does not love them any less but much more deeply than before.

Numbered among them are the pure and authentic achievements of art and science. In a much more general way they include everything that envelops human life with poetry through the various social strata. Every human being has at his roots here below a certain terrestrial poetry, a reflection of the heavenly glory, the link, of which he is more or less vaguely conscious, with his universal country. Affliction is the tearing up of these roots.

Human cities in particular, each one more or less according to its degree of perfection, surround the life of their inhabitants with poetry. They are images and reflections of the city of the world. Actually, the more they have the form of a nation, the more they claim to be countries themselves, the more distorted and soiled they are as images. But to destroy cities, either materially or morally, or to exclude human beings from a city, thrusting them down to the state of social outcasts, this is to sever every bond of poetry and love between human beings and the universe. It is to plunge them forcibly into the horror of ugliness. There can scarcely be a greater crime. We all have a share by our complicity in an almost innumerable quantity of such crimes. If only we could understand, it should wring tears of blood from us.

THE LOVE OF RELIGIOUS PRACTICES

The love of institutional religion, although the name of God necessarily comes into it, is not in itself an explicit, but an implicit love of God, for it does not involve direct, immediate contact with him. God is present in religious practices, when they are pure, just as he is present in our neighbor and in the beauty of the world; in the same way and not any more.

The form that the love of religion takes in the soul differs a great deal according to the circumstances of our lives. Some circumstances prevent the very birth of this love; others kill it before it has been able to grow very strong. In affliction some men, in spite of themselves, develop a hatred and contempt for religion because the cruelty, pride, or corruption of certain of its ministers have made them suffer.

There are others who have been reared from their earliest youth in surroundings impregnated with a spirit of this sort. We must conclude that in such cases, by God's mercy, the love of our neighbor and the love of the beauty of the world, if they are sufficiently strong and pure, will be enough to raise the soul to any height.

The love of institutional religion normally has as its object the prevailing religion of the country or circle in which a man is brought up. As the result of an inborn habit, everyone thinks first of that each time he thinks of a religious service.

The whole virtue of religious practices can be conceived of from the Buddhist tradition concerning the recitation of the name of the Lord. It is said that Buddha made a vow to raise to himself, in the Land of Purity, all those who pronounced his name with the desire of being saved by him; and that because of this vow the recitation of the name of the Lord really has the power of transforming the soul.

Religion is nothing else but this promise of God. Every religious practice, every rite, all liturgy is a form of the recitation of the name of the Lord and in principle should have a real virtue, the virtue of saving whoever devotes himself to performing it with desire.

All religions pronounce the name of God in their particular language. As a rule it is better for a man to name God in his native tongue rather than in one that is foreign to him. Except in special cases the soul is not able to abandon itself utterly when it has to make the slight effort of seeking for the words in a foreign language, even when this language is well known.

A writer whose native language is poor, difficult to manipulate, and not widely known throughout the world is very strongly tempted to adopt another. There are a few like Conrad who have done so with startling success. But they are very rare. Except in special cases such a change does harm, both thought and style suffer, the writer is always ill at ease in the adopted language and cannot rise above mediocrity.

A change of religion is for the soul like a change of language for a writer. All religions, it is true, are not equally suitable for the recitation of the name of the Lord. Some, without any doubt, are very imperfect mediums. The religion of Israel, for instance, must have been imperfect when it made the crucifixion of Christ possible. The Roman religion can scarcely be said to deserve the name of religion at all.

But in general the relative value of the various religions is a very difficult thing to discern; it is almost impossible, perhaps quite impossible. For a religion is known only from inside. Catholics say this of Catholicism, but it is true of all religions. Religion is a form of nourishment. It is difficult to appreciate the flavor and food value of something one has never eaten.

The comparison of religions is only possible, in some measure, through the miraculous virtue of sympathy. We can know men to a certain extent if at the same time as we observe them from outside we manage by sympathy to transport our own soul into theirs for a time. In the same way the study of different religions does not lead to a real knowledge of them unless we transport ourselves for a time by faith to the very center of whichever one we are studying. Here, moreover, this word faith is used in its strongest sense.

This scarcely ever happens, for some have no faith, and the others have faith exclusively in one religion and only bestow upon the others the sort of attention we give to strangely shaped shells. There are others again who think they are capable of impartiality because they have only a vague religiosity which they can turn indifferently in any direction, whereas, on the contrary, we must have given all our attention, all our faith, all our love to a particular religion in order to think of any other religion with the high degree of attention, faith, and love that is proper to it. In the same way, only those who are capable of friendship can take a real heartfelt interest in the fate of an utter stranger.

In all departments of life, love is not real unless it is directed toward a particular object; it becomes universal without ceasing to be real only as a result of analogy and transference.

It might be said in passing that the knowledge of what analogy and transference are, a knowledge for which mathematics, the various branches of science, and philosophy are a preparation, also has a direct relationship to love.

In Europe today, and perhaps even in the whole world, the knowledge of comparative religion amounts to just about nothing. People have not even a notion of the possibility of such a knowledge. Even without the prejudices which get in our way, it is already very difficult for us even to form an idea of it. Among the different forms of religion there are, as it were, partial compensations for the visible differences, certain hidden equivalents which can only be caught sight of by the most penetrating discernment. Each religion is an original combination of explicit and implicit truths; what is explicit in one is implicit in another. The implicit adherence to a truth can in some cases be worth as much as the explicit adherence, sometimes even a great deal more. He who knows the secrets of all hearts alone knows the secret of the different forms of faith. He has never revealed this secret, whatever anyone may say.

If one is born into a religion which is not too unsuitable for pronouncing the name of the Lord, if one loves this native religion with a well directed and pure love, it is difficult to imagine a legitimate motive for giving it up, before direct contact with God has placed the soul under the guidance of the divine will itself. After that the change is only legitimate if it is made in obedience. History shows that in fact this happens but rarely. Most often, perhaps always, the soul that has reached the highest realms of spirituality is confirmed in its love of the tradition that served it as a ladder.

If the imperfection of the religion in which one is born is too great, or if the form under which it appears in one's native surroundings is too corrupt, or if, through special circumstances, love for this religion has never been born or has been killed, the adoption of a foreign religion is legitimate. It is legitimate and necessary for certain people; probably not for everybody. This is the same with regard to those who have been brought up without the practice of any religion.

In all other cases, to change one's religion is a very serious decision, and it is much more serious to influence another person to change. It is yet more, infinitely more serious to exercise official pressure of such a nature in a conquered country.

On the other hand, in spite of all the varieties of religion existing in Europe and America, one might say that in principle, directly or indirectly, closely or only from afar, the Catholic religion forms the native spiritual background of all men belonging to the white races.

The virtue of religious practices is due to a contact with what is perfectly pure, resulting in the destruction of evil. Nothing here below is perfectly pure except the total beauty of the universe, and that we are unable to feel directly until we are very far advanced in the way of perfection. Moreover, this total beauty cannot be contained in anything tangible, though it is itself tangible in a certain sense.

Religious things are special tangible things, existing here below and yet perfectly pure. This is not on account of their own particular character. The church may be ugly, the singing out of tune, the priest corrupt, and the faithful inattentive. In a sense that is of no importance. It is as with a geometrician who draws a figure to illustrate a proof. If the lines are not straight and the circles are not round it is of no importance. Religious things are pure by right, theoretically, hypothetically, by convention. Therefore their purity is unconditioned. No stain can sully it. That is why it is perfect. It is not, however, perfect in the same way as Roland's mare, which, while it had all possible virtues, had also the drawback of not existing. Human conventions are useless if they are not connected with motives that impel people to observe them. In themselves they are simple abstractions; they are unreal and have no effect. But the convention by which religious things are pure is ratified by God himself. Thus it is an effective convention, a convention containing virtue and operating of itself. This purity is unconditioned and perfect, and at the same time real.

There we have a truth that is a fact and in consequence cannot be demonstrated by argument. It can only be verified experimentally.

It is a fact that the purity of religious things is almost everywhere to be seen in the form of beauty, when faith and love do not fail. Thus the words of the liturgy are marvelously beautiful; and the words of the prayer issued for us from the very lips of Christ is perfect above all. In the same way Romanesque architecture and Gregorian plain chant are marvelously beautiful.

At the very center, however, there is something utterly stripped of beauty, where there is no outward evidence of purity, something depending wholly on convention. It cannot be otherwise. Architecture, singing, language, even if the words are chosen by Christ himself, all those things are in a sense distinct from absolute purity. Absolute purity, present here below to our earthly senses, as a particular thing, such can only be a convention, which is a convention and nothing else. This convention, placed at the central point, is the Eucharist.

The virtue of the dogma of the real presence lies in its very absurdity. Except for the infinitely touching symbolism of food, there is nothing in a morsel of bread that can be associated with our thought of God. Thus the conventional character of the divine presence is evident. Christ can be present in such an object only by convention. For this very reason he can be perfectly present in it. God can only be present in secret here below. His presence in the Eucharist is truly secret since no part of our thought can reach the secret. Thus it is total.

No one dreams of being surprised that reasoning worked out from nonexistent perfect lines and perfect circles should be effectively applied to engineering. Yet that is incomprehensible. The reality of the divine presence in the Eucharist is more marvelous but not more incomprehensible.

One might in a sense say by analogy that Christ is present in the consecrated host by hypothesis, in the same way that a geometrician says by hypothesis that there are two equal angles in a certain triangle.

It is because it has to do with a convention that only the form of the consecration matters, not the spiritual state of him who consecrates.

If it were something other than a convention, it would be at least partially human and not totally divine. A real convention is a supernatural harmony, taking the word harmony in the Pythagorean sense.

Only a convention can be the perfection of purity here below, for all nonconventional purity is more or less imperfect. That a convention should be real, that is a miracle of divine mercy.

The Buddhist conception of the recitation of the name of the Lord contains the same truth, for a name is a convention too. Yet our habit of thought which confuses things with their names makes us forget this very easily. The Eucharist is conventional to a higher degree.

Even the presence of Christ in human flesh was something other than perfect purity, since he censured the man who called him good, and since he said: "It is expedient for you that I go away." * He must then be more completely present in a morsel of consecrated bread. His presence is more complete inasmuch as it is more secret.

Yet this presence was probably still more complete, and also still more secret, in his body of flesh at the moment when the police seized this body as that of a common criminal. But as a result he was forsaken by all. He was too present. Men could not endure it.

The convention of the Eucharist, or something of the kind, is indispensable for man; the presence of perfect purity is indispensable for him. For man can only fix his full attention on something tangible, and he needs sometimes to fix his attention upon perfect purity. Only this act can make it possible for him, by a process of transference, to destroy a part of the evil that is in him. That is why the Host is really the Lamb of God which takes away sin.

We are all conscious of evil within ourselves; we all have a horror of it and want to get rid of it. Outside ourselves we see evil under two distinct forms, suffering and sin. But in our feelings about our own nature the distinction no longer appears, except abstractly or through reflection. We feel in ourselves something which is neither suffering nor sin, which is the two of them at once, the root common to both,

* John 16:7.

189

defilement and pain at the same time. This is the presence of evil in us. It is the ugliness in us. The more we feel it, the more it fills us with horror. The soul rejects it in the same way as we vomit. By a process of transference we pass it on to the things that surround us. These things, however, thus becoming blemished and ugly in our eyes, send us back the evil that we had put into them. They send it back after adding to it. In this exchange the evil in us increases. It seems to us then that the very places where we are living and the things that surround us imprison us in evil, and that it becomes daily worse. This is a terrible anguish. When the soul, worn out with this anguish, ceases to feel it any more, there is little hope of its salvation.

It is thus that an invalid conceives hatred and disgust for his room and surroundings, a prisoner for his cell, and only too often a worker for his factory.

It is useless to provide people in this state with beautiful things, for there is nothing which does not eventually become spoiled and sullied by this process of transference, until it ends up as an object of horror.

Perfect purity alone cannot be defiled. If at the moment when the soul is invaded by evil the attention can be turned toward a thing of perfect purity, so that a part of the evil is transferred to it, this thing will be in no way tarnished by it, nor will it send it back. Thus each minute of such attention really destroys a part of the evil.

What the Hebrews tried to accomplish, by means of a kind of magic, in their rite of the scapegoat, can only be carried out here on earth by perfect purity. The true scapegoat is the Lamb.

The day when a perfect being was to be found here below in human form, the greatest possible amount of evil scattered around him was automatically concentrated upon him in the form of suffering. At that time, throughout the Roman Empire, the greatest misfortune and the greatest crime among men was slavery. That is why he suffered the death which was the extremity of affliction possible for a slave. In a mysterious manner this transference constitutes the Redemption.

It is the same when a human being turns his eyes and his attention toward the Lamb of God present in the consecrated bread, a part of the evil which he bears within him is directed toward perfect purity, and there suffers destruction.

It is a transmutation rather than a destruction. The contact with perfect purity dissociates the suffering and sin which had been mixed together so indissolubly. The part of evil in the soul is burned by the fire of this contact and becomes only suffering, and the suffering is impregnated with love.

In the same way when all the evil diffused throughout the Roman Empire was concentrated on Christ it became only suffering to him.

If there were not perfect and infinite purity here below, if there were only finite purity, which contact with evil eventually exhausts, we could never be saved.

Penal justice affords a frightful illustration of this truth. In principle it is something pure which has goodness for its object. It is, however, an imperfect, finite, human purity. Therefore, uninterrupted contact with a mixture of crime and affliction wears away this purity and puts in its place a defilement about equal to the totality of crime, a defilement far exceeding that of any particular criminal.

Men fail to drink from the source of purity. Creation would however be an act of cruelty if this spring did not well up wherever there is crime and affliction. If there had been no crime and affliction in the centuries further back than two thousand years, and in the countries untouched by missions, we might think that the Church had the monopoly of Christ and the sacraments. How can we bear the thought of a single crucified slave twenty-two centuries ago, how can we help accusing God, if we think that at that time Christ was absent and every kind of sacrament unknown? It is true that we hardly think at all about slaves crucified twenty-two centuries ago.

When we have learned to look at perfect purity, the shortness of human life is the only thing to prevent us from being sure that unless we play false we can attain perfection even here on earth. For we are finite beings and the evil that is within us is finite too. The purity that is offered to our eyes is infinite. However little evil we were to destroy at each look, we could be certain, if our time were unlimited that by looking often enough, one day we should destroy it all. We should then have reached the end of evil as the *Bhagavad-Gita* expresses so magnificently. We should have destroyed evil for the Lord of Truth and we should bring him truth, as the Egyptian Book of the Dead says.

One of the principal truths of Christianity, a truth that goes almost unrecognized today, is that looking is what saves us. The bronze serpent was lifted up so that those who lay maimed in the depths of degradation should be saved by looking upon it.

It is at those moments when we are, as we say, in a bad mood, when we feel incapable of the elevation of soul that befits holy things, it is then that it is most effectual to turn our eyes toward perfect purity. For it is then that evil, or rather mediocrity, comes to the surface of the soul and is in the best position for being burned by contact with the fire.

It is however then that the act of looking is almost impossible. All the mediocre part of the soul, fearing death with a more violent fear than that caused by the approach of the death of the body, revolts and suggests lies to protect itself.

The effort not to listen to these lies, although we cannot prevent ourselves from believing them, the effort to look upon purity at such times, has to be something very violent; yet it is absolutely different from all that is generally known as effort, such as doing violence to one's feelings or an act of will. Other words are needed to express it, but language cannot provide them.

The effort that brings a soul to salvation is like the effort of looking or of listening; it is the kind of effort by which a fiancée accepts her lover. It is an act of attention and consent; whereas what language designates as will is something suggestive of muscular effort.

The will is on the level of the natural part of the soul. The right use of the will is a condition of salvation, necessary no doubt but remote, inferior, very subordinate and purely negative. The weeds are pulled up by the muscular effort of the peasant, but only sun and water can make the corn grow. The will cannot produce any good in the soul.

Compare w/ Augustine

Efforts of the will are only in their right place for carrying out definite obligations. Wherever there is no strict obligation we must follow either our natural inclination or our vocation, that is to say God's command. Actions prompted by our inclination clearly do not involve an effort of will. In our acts of obedience to God we are passive; whatever difficulties we have to surmount, however great our activity may appear to be, there is nothing analogous to muscular effort; there is only waiting, attention, silence, immobility, constant through suffering and joy. The crucifixion of Christ is the model of all acts of obedience.

This kind of passive activity, the highest of all, is perfectly described in the *Bhagavad-Gita* and in Lao-Tse. Also there is a supernatural union of opposites, harmony in the Pythagorean sense.

That we have to strive after goodness with an effort of our will is one of the lies invented by the mediocre part of ourselves in its fear of being destroyed. Such an effort does not threaten it in any way, it does not even disturb its comfort—not even when it entails a great deal of fatigue and suffering. For the mediocre part of ourselves is not afraid of fatigue and suffering; it is afraid of being killed.

There are people who try to raise their souls like a man continually taking standing jumps in the hopes that, if he jumps higher every day, a time may come when he will no longer fall back but will go right up to the sky. Thus occupied he cannot look at the sky. We cannot take a single step toward heaven. It is not in our power to travel in a vertical direction. If however we look heavenward for a long time, God comes and takes us up. He raises us easily.

As Aeschylus says: "There is no effort in what is divine." There is an easiness in salvation which is more difficult to us than all our efforts.

In one of Grimm's stories there is a competition between a giant and a little tailor to see which is the stronger. The giant throws a stone so high that it takes a very long time before it comes down again. The little tailor lets a bird fly and it does not come down at all. Anything without wings always comes down again in the end.

It is because the will has no power to bring about salvation that the idea of secular morality is an absurdity. What is called morality only depends on the will in what is, so to speak, its most muscular aspect. Religion on the contrary corresponds to desire, and it is desire that saves.

The Roman caricature of Stoicism also appeals to the muscular will. But true Stoicism, the Stoicism of the Greeks, from which Saint John, or perhaps Christ, borrowed the terms "*Logos*" and "*pneuma*," is purely desire, piety, and love. It is full of humility.

The Christianity of today has let itself become contaminated by its adversaries, on this point as on many others. The metaphor of a search for God is suggestive of efforts of muscular will. It is true that Pascal contributed to the spread of this metaphor. He made several mistakes, notably that of confusing faith and autosuggestion to a certain extent.

In the great symbols of mythology and folklore, in the parables of the Gospel, it is God who seeks man. "*Quaerens me sedisti lassus.*" Nowhere in the Gospel is there question of a search undertaken by man. Man does not take a step unless he receives some pressure or is definitely called. The role of the future wife is to wait. The slave waits and watches while his master is at a festival. The passer-by does not invite himself to the marriage feast, he does not ask for an invitation; he is brought in almost by surprise; his part is only to put on the appropriate garment. The man who has found a pearl in a field sells all his goods to buy the field; he does not need to dig up the whole field with a spade in order to unearth the pearl; it is enough for him to sell all he possesses. To long for God and to renounce all the rest, that alone can save us.

The attitude that brings about salvation is not like any form of activity. The Greek word which expresses it is ὑπομενή, and *patientia* is rather an inadequate translation of it. It is the waiting or attentive and faithful immobility that lasts indefinitely and cannot be shaken. The slave, who waits near the door so as to open immediately the master knocks, is the best image of it. He must be ready to die of hunger and exhaustion rather than change his attitude. It must be possible for his companions to call him, talk to him, hit him, without his even turning his head. Even if he is told that the master is dead, and even if he believes it, he will not move. If he is told that the master is angry with him and will beat him when he returns, and if he believes it, he will not move.

Active searching is prejudicial, not only to love, but also to the intelligence, whose laws are the same as those of love. We just have to wait for the solution of a geometrical problem or the meaning of a Latin or Greek sentence to come into our mind. Still more must we wait for any new scientific truth or for a beautiful line of poetry. Seeking leads us astray. This is the case with every form of what is truly good. Man should do nothing but wait for the good and keep evil away. He should make no muscular effort except in order not to be shaken by evil. In the constant turning and returning of which our human condition is made up, true virtue in every domain is negative, at least in appearance. This waiting for goodness and truth is, however, something more intense than any searching.

The notion of grace, as opposed to virtue depending on the will, and that of inspiration, as opposed to intellectual or artistic work, these two notions, if they are well understood, show the efficacy of desire and of waiting.

Attention animated by desire is the whole foundation of religious practices. That is why no system of morality can take their place. The mediocre part of the soul has, however, a great many lies in its arsenal that are capable of protecting it, even during prayer or the participation of the sacraments. It puts veils between our eyes and the presence of perfect purity, and it is clever enough to call them God— such veils, for instance, as states of the soul, sources of sensible joy, of hope, of comfort, of soothing consolation, or else a combination of habits, or one or several human beings, or perhaps a social circle.

It is difficult to avoid the pitfall of striving to imagine the divine perfection religion invites us to love. Never in any case can we imagine something more perfect than ourselves. This effort renders useless the marvel of the Eucharist.

A certain formation of the intelligence is necessary in order to be able to contemplate in the Eucharist only what by definition it enshrines, that is to say, something which is totally outside our experience, something of which we only know, as Plato says, that it exists and that nothing else can ever be desired except in error.

The trap of traps, the almost inevitable trap, is the social one. Everywhere, always, in everything, the social feeling produces a perfect imitation of faith, that is to say perfectly deceptive. This imitation has the great advantage of satisfying every part of the soul. That which longs for goodness believes it is fed. That which is mediocre is not hurt by the light; it is quite at its ease. Thus everyone is in agreement. The soul is at peace. But Christ said that he did not come to bring peace. He brought a sword, the sword that severs in two, as Aeschylus says.

It is almost impossible to distinguish faith from its social imitation. All the more so because the soul can contain one part of true faith and one of imitation faith. It is almost but not quite impossible.

Under present circumstances, it is perhaps a question of life or death for faith that the social imitation should be repudiated.

The necessity for a perfectly pure presence to take away defilement is not restricted to churches. People come with their stains to the churches, and that is all very well. It would, however, be more in conformity with the spirit of Christianity if, besides that, Christ went to bring his presence into those places most polluted with shame, misery, crime, and affliction, into prisons and law courts, into work-houses and shelters for the wretched and the outcast. Every session of bench or courts should begin and end with a prayer, in which the magistrates, the police, the accused, and the public shared. Christ should not be absent from the places where work or study is going on. All human beings, whatever they are doing and wherever they are, should be able to have their eyes fixed, during the whole of each day, upon the serpent of bronze.

It should also be publicly and officially recognized that religion is nothing else but a looking. In so far as it claims to be anything else, it is inevitable that it should either be shut up inside churches, or that it should stifle everything in every other place where it is found. Religion should not claim to occupy a place in society other than that which rightly belongs to supernatural love in the soul. Moreover it is true also that many people degrade charity in themselves because they want to make it occupy too large and too visible a place in their soul. Our Father lives only in secret. Love should always be accompanied by modesty. True faith implies great discretion, even with regard to itself. It is a secret between God and us in which we ourselves have scarcely any part.

The love of our neighbor, the love of the beauty of the world, and the love of religion are in a sense quite impersonal loves. This could easily not be so in the last case, because religion is connected with a certain section of society. The very nature of religious practices must remedy this. At the center of the Catholic religion a little formless matter is found, a little piece of bread. The love directed toward this particle of matter is necessarily impersonal. It is not the human person of Christ such as we picture him; it is not the divine person of the Father, likewise subject to

all the errors of our imagination; it is outwardly only a fragment of matter, yet it is at the center of the Catholic
religion. Herein lies the great scandal and yet the most
wonderful virtue of this religion. In all authentic forms of
religious life alike, there is something that guarantees their
impersonal character. The love of God ought to be impersonal as long as there has not been any direct and personal
contact; otherwise it is an imaginary love. Afterward it
ought to be both personal and impersonal again, but this
time in a higher sense.

FRIENDSHIP

There is however a personal and human love which is
pure and which enshrines an intimation and a reflection of
divine love. This is friendship, provided we keep strictly to
the true meaning of the word.

Preference for some human being is necessarily a different thing from charity. Charity does not discriminate. If it
is found more abundantly in any special quarter, it is because affliction has chanced to provide an occasion there for
the exchange of compassion and gratitude. It is equally
available for the whole human race, inasmuch as affliction
can come to all, offering them an opportunity for such an
exchange.

Preference for a human being can be of two kinds. Either
we are seeking some particular good in him, or we need him.
In a general way all possible attachments come under one of
these heads. We are drawn toward a thing, either because
there is some good we are seeking from it, or because we

cannot do without it. Sometimes the two motives coincide. Often however they do not. Each is distinct and quite independent. We eat distasteful food, if we have nothing else, because we cannot do otherwise. A moderately greedy man looks out for delicacies, but he can easily do without them. If we have no air we are suffocated; we struggle to get it, not because we expect to get some advantage from it but because we need it. We go in search of sea air without being driven by any necessity, because we like it. In time it often comes about automatically that the second motive takes the place of the first. This is one of the great misfortunes of our race. A man smokes opium in order to attain to a special condition, which he thinks superior; often, as time goes on, the opium reduces him to a miserable condition which he feels to be degrading, but he is no longer able to do without it. Arnolphe bought Agnes * from her adopted mother, because it seemed to him it would be an advantage to have a little girl with him, a little girl whom he would gradually make into a good wife. Later on she ceased to cause him anything but a heart-rending and degrading torment. But with the passage of time his attachment to her had become a vital bond which forced this terrible line from his lips:

"*Mais je sens là-dedans qu'il faudra que je crève—*" †

Harpagon started by considering gold as an advantage. Later it became nothing but the object of a haunting obsession, yet an object of which the loss would cause his death. As Plato says, there is a great difference between the essence of the Necessary and that of the Good.

* Characters in Molière's *L'Ecole des Femmes*. Harpagon, below, is a character in Molière's *L'Avare*.

† But I feel in all this that I shall be torn asunder.

There is no contradiction between seeking our own good in a human being and wishing for his good to be increased. For this very reason, when the motive that draws us toward anybody is simply some advantage for ourselves, the conditions of friendship are not fulfilled. Friendship is a supernatural harmony, a union of opposites.

When a human being is in any degree necessary to us, we cannot desire his good unless we cease to desire our own. Where there is necessity there is constraint and domination. We are in the power of that of which we stand in need, unless we possess it. The central good for every man is the free disposal of himself. Either we renounce it, which is a crime of idolatry, since it can be renounced only in favor of God, or we desire that the being we stand in need of should be deprived of this free disposal of himself.

Any kind of mechanism may join human beings together with bonds of affection which have the iron hardness of necessity. Mother love is often of such a kind; so at times is paternal love, as in *Père Goriot* of Balzac; so is carnal love in its most intense form, as in *L'Ecole des Femmes* and in *Phèdre*; so also, very frequently, is the love between husband and wife, chiefly as a result of habit. Filial and fraternal love are more rarely of this nature.

There are moreover degrees of necessity. Everything is necessary in some degree if its loss really causes a decrease of vital energy. (This word is here used in the strict and precise sense that it might have if the study of vital phenomena were as far advanced as that of falling bodies.) When the degree of necessity is extreme, deprivation leads to death. This is the case when all the vital energy of one being is bound up with another by some attachment. In the lesser degrees, deprivation leads to a more or less considerable lessening of energy. Thus a total deprivation of food causes death, whereas a partial deprivation only diminishes the life force. Nevertheless the necessary quantity of food is considered to be that required if a person is not to be weakened.

The most frequent cause of necessity in the bonds of affection is a combination of sympathy and habit. As in the case of avarice or drunkenness, that which was at first a search for some desired good is transformed into a need by the mere passage of time. The difference from avarice, drunkenness, and all the vices, however, is that in the bonds of affection the two motives—search for a desired good, and need—can very easily coexist. They can also be separated. When the attachment of one being to another is made up of need and nothing else it is a fearful thing. Few things in this world can reach such a degree of ugliness and horror. There is always something horrible whenever a human being seeks what is good and only finds necessity. The stories that tell of a beloved being who suddenly appears with a death's head best symbolize this. The human soul possesses a whole arsenal of lies with which to put up a defense against this ugliness and, in imagination, to manufacture sham advantages where there is only necessity. It is for this very reason that ugliness is an evil, because it conduces to lying.

Speaking quite generally, we might say that there is affliction whenever necessity, under no matter what form, is imposed so harshly that the hardness exceeds the capacity for lying of the person who receives the impact. That is why the purest souls are the most exposed to affliction. For him who is capable of preventing the automatic reaction of defense, which tends to increase the soul's capacity for lying, affliction is not an evil, although it is always a wounding and in a sense a degradation.

When a human being is attached to another by a bond of affection which contains any degree of necessity, it is impossible that he should wish autonomy to be preserved both in himself and in the other. It is impossible by virtue of the mechanism of nature. It is, however, made possible by the miraculous intervention of the supernatural. This miracle is friendship.

"Friendship is an equality made of harmony," said the Pythagoreans. There is harmony because there is a supernatural union between two opposites, that is to say, necessity and liberty, the two opposites God combined when he created the world and men. There is equality because each wishes to preserve the faculty of free consent both in himself and in the other.

When anyone wishes to put himself under a human being or consents to be subordinated to him, there is no trace of friendship. Racine's Pylades is not the friend of Orestes. There is no friendship where there is inequality.

A certain reciprocity is essential in friendship. If all good will is entirely lacking on one of the two sides, the other should suppress his own affection, out of respect for the free consent which he should not desire to force. If on one of the two sides there is not any respect for the autonomy of the other, this other must cut the bond uniting them out of respect for himself. In the same way, he who consents to be enslaved cannot gain friendship. But the necessity contained in the bond of affection can exist on one side only, and in this case there is only friendship on one side, if we keep to the strict and exact meaning of the word.

A friendship is tarnished as soon as necessity triumphs, if only for a moment, over the desire to preserve the faculty of free consent on both sides. In all human things, necessity is the principle of impurity. All friendship is impure if even a trace of the wish to please or the contrary desire to dominate is found in it. In a perfect friendship these two desires are completely absent. The two friends have fully consented to be two and not one, they respect the distance which the fact of being two distinct creatures places between them. Man has the right to desire direct union with God alone.

Friendship is a miracle by which a person consents to view from a certain distance, and without coming any nearer, the very being who is necessary to him as food. It requires the strength of soul that Eve did not have; and yet she had no need of the fruit. If she had been hungry at the moment when she looked at the fruit, and if in spite of that she had remained looking at it indefinitely without taking one step toward it, she would have performed a miracle analogous to that of perfect friendship.

Through this supernatural miracle of respect for human autonomy, friendship is very like the pure forms of compassion and gratitude called forth by affliction. In both cases the contraries which are the terms of the harmony are necessity and liberty, or in other words subordination and equality. These two pairs of opposites are equivalent.

From the fact that the desire to please and the desire to command are not found in pure friendship, it has in it, at the same time as affection, something not unlike a complete indifference. Although it is a bond between two people it is in a sense impersonal. It leaves impartiality intact. It in no way prevents us from imitating the perfection of our Father in heaven who freely distributes sunlight and rain in every place. On the contrary, friendship and this distribution are the mutual conditions one of the other, in most cases at any rate. For, as practically every human being is joined to others by bonds of affection that have in them some degree of necessity, he cannot go toward perfection except by transforming this affection into friendship. Friendship has something universal about it. It consists of loving a human being as we should like to be able to love each soul in particular of all those who go to make up the human race. As a geometrician looks at a particular figure in order to deduce the universal properties of the triangle, so he who knows how to love directs upon a particular human being a universal love. The consent to preserve an autonomy within ourselves and in others is essentially of a universal order. As soon as we wish for this autonomy to be respected in more than just one single being we desire it for everyone, for we cease to arrange the order of the world in a circle whose center is here below. We transport the center of the circle beyond the heavens.

Friendship does not have this power if the two beings who love each other, through an unlawful use of affection, think they form only one. But then there is not friendship in the true sense of the word. That is what might be called an adulterous union, even though it comes about between husband and wife. There is not friendship where distance is not kept and respected.

The simple fact of having pleasure in thinking in the same way as the beloved being, or in any case the fact of desiring such an agreement of opinion, attacks the purity of the friendship at the same time as its intellectual integrity. It is very frequent. But at the same time pure friendship is rare.

When the bonds of affection and necessity between human beings are not supernaturally transformed into friendship, not only is the affection of an impure and low order, but it is also combined with hatred and repulsion. That is shown very well in *L'Ecole des Femmes* and in *Phèdre*. The mechanism is the same in affections other than carnal love. It is easy to understand this. We hate what we are dependent upon. We become disgusted with what depends on us. Sometimes affection does not only become mixed with hatred and revulsion; it is entirely changed into it. The transformation may sometimes even be almost immediate, so that hardly any affection has had time to show; this is the case when necessity is laid bare almost at once. When the necessity which brings people together has nothing to do with the emotions, when it is simply due to circumstances, hostility often makes its appearance from the start.

When Christ said to his disciples: "Love one another," it was not attachment he was laying down as their rule. As it was a fact that there were bonds between them due to the thoughts, the life, and the habits they shared, he commanded them to transform these bonds into friendship, so that they should not be allowed to turn into impure attachment or hatred.

Since, shortly before his death, Christ gave this as a new commandment to be added to the two great commandments of the love of our neighbor and the love of God, we can think that pure friendship, like the love of our neighbor, has in it something of a sacrament. Christ perhaps wished to suggest this with reference to Christian friendship when he said: "Where there are two or three gathered together in my name there am I in the midst of them." Pure friendship is an image of the original and perfect friendship that belongs to the Trinity and is the very essence of God. It is impossible for two human beings to be one while scrupulously respecting the distance that separates them, unless God is present in each of them. The point at which parallels meet is infinity.

IMPLICIT AND EXPLICIT LOVE

Even the most narrow-minded of Catholics would not dare to affirm that compassion, gratitude, love of the beauty of the world, love of religious practices, and friendship belonged exclusively to those centuries and countries that recognized the Church. These forms of love are rarely found in their purity, but it would even be difficult to say that they were met with more frequently in those centuries and countries than in the others. To think that love in any of these forms can exist anywhere where Christ is absent is to belittle him so grievously that it amounts to an outrage. It is impious and almost sacrilegious.

These kinds of love are supernatural, and in a sense they are absurd. They are the height of folly. So long as the soul has not had direct contact with the very person of God, they cannot be supported by any knowledge based either on experience or reason. They cannot therefore rest upon any certainty, unless the word is used in a metaphorical sense to indicate the opposite of hesitation. In consequence it is better that they should not be associated with any belief. This is more honest intellectually, and it safeguards our love's purity more effectively. On this account it is more fitting. In what concerns divine things, belief is not fitting. Only certainty will do. Anything less than certainty is unworthy of God.

During the period of preparation, these indirect loves constitute an upward movement of the soul, a turning of the eyes, not without some effort, toward higher things. After God has come in person, not only to visit the soul as he does for a long time beforehand, but to possess it and to transport its center near to his very heart, it is otherwise. The chicken has cracked its shell; it is outside the egg of the world. These first loves continue; they are more intense than before, but they are different. He who has passed through this adventure has a deeper love than ever for those who suffer affliction and for those who help him in his own, for his friends, for religious practices, and for the beauty of the world. But his love in all these forms has become a movement of God himself, a ray merged in the light of God. That at least is what we may suppose.

These indirect loves are only the attitude toward beings and things here below of the soul turned toward the Good.

They themselves have not any particular good as an object. There is no final good here below. Thus strictly speaking we are no longer concerned with forms of love, but with attitudes inspired by love.

In the period of preparation the soul loves in emptiness. It does not know whether anything real answers its love. It may believe that it knows, but to believe is not to know. Such a belief does not help. The soul knows for certain only that it is hungry. The important thing is that it announces its hunger by crying. A child does not stop crying if we suggest to it that perhaps there is no bread. It goes on crying just the same.

The danger is not lest the soul should doubt whether there is any bread, but lest, by a lie, it should persuade itself that it is not hungry. It can only persuade itself of this by lying, for the reality of its hunger is not a belief, it is a certainty.

We all know that there is no true good here below, that everything that appears to be good in this world is finite, limited, wears out, and once worn out, leaves necessity exposed in all its nakedness. Every human being has probably had some lucid moments in his life when he has definitely acknowledged to himself that there is no final good here below. But as soon as we have seen this truth we cover it up with lies. Many people even take pleasure in proclaiming it, seeking a morbid joy in their sadness, without ever having been able to bear facing it for a second. Men feel that there is a mortal danger in facing this truth squarely for any length of time. That is true. Such knowledge strikes more surely than a sword; it inflicts a death more frightening than that of the body. After a time it kills everything within us that constitutes our ego. In order to bear it we have to love truth more than life itself. Those who do this turn away from the fleeting things of time with all their souls, to use the expression of Plato.

They do not turn toward God. How could they do so when they are in total darkness? God himself sets their faces in the right direction. He does not, however, show himself to them for a long time. It is for them to remain motionless, without averting their eyes, listening ceaselessly, and waiting, they know not for what; deaf to entreaties and threats, unmoved by every shock, unshaken in the midst of every upheaval. If after a long period of waiting God allows them to have an indistinct intuition of his light or even reveals himself in person, it is only for an instant. Once more they have to remain still, attentive, inactive, calling out only when their desire cannot be contained.

It does not rest with the soul to believe in the reality of God if God does not reveal this reality. In trying to do so it either labels something else with the name of God, and that is idolatry, or else its belief in God remains abstract and verbal. Such a belief prevails wherever religious dogma is taken for granted, as is the case with those centuries and countries in which it never enters anyone's head to question it. The state of nonbelief is then what Saint John of the Cross calls a night. The belief is verbal and does not penetrate the soul. At a time like the present, incredulity may be equivalent to the dark night of Saint John of the Cross if the unbeliever loves God, if he is like the child who does not know whether there is bread anywhere, but who cries out because he is hungry.

When we are eating bread, and even when we have eaten it, we know that it is real. We can nevertheless raise doubts about the reality of the bread. Philosophers raise doubts about the reality of the world of the senses. Such doubts are however purely verbal; they leave the certainty intact and actually serve only to make it more obvious to a well-balanced mind. In the same way he to whom God has revealed his reality can raise doubts about this reality without any harm. They are purely verbal doubts, a form of exercise to keep his intelligence in good health. What amounts to criminal treason, even before such a revelation and much more afterward, is to question the fact that God is the only thing worthy of love. That is a turning away of our eyes, for love is the soul's looking. It means that we have stopped for an instant to wait and to listen.

Electra did not seek Orestes, she waited for him. When she was convinced that he no longer existed, and that nowhere in the whole world was there anything that could be Orestes, she did not on that account return to her former associates. She drew back from them with greater aversion than ever. She preferred the absence of Orestes to the presence of anyone else. Orestes was to have delivered her from slavery, from rags, servile work, dirt, hunger, blows, and innumerable humiliations. She no longer hoped for that. But never for an instant did she dream of employing another method which could obtain a luxurious and honored life for her—the method of reconciliation with those in power. She did not want wealth and consideration unless they came through Orestes. She did not even give a thought to such things. All she wanted was to exist no longer, since Orestes had ceased to exist.

At that moment Orestes could hold out no longer. He could not help declaring himself. He gave certain proof that he was Orestes. Electra saw him, she heard him, she touched him. There would be no more question for her now as to whether her savior was in existence.

He who has had the same adventure as Electra, he whose soul has seen, heard, and touched for itself, he will recognize God as the reality inspiring all indirect loves, the reality of which they are as it were the reflections. God is pure beauty. This is incomprehensible, for beauty, by its very essence, has to do with the senses. To speak of an imperceptible beauty must seem a misuse of language to anyone who has any sense of exactitude: and with reason. Beauty is always a miracle. But the miracle is raised to the second degree when the soul receives an impression of beauty which, while it is beyond all sense perception is no abstraction, but real and direct as the impression caused by a song at the moment it reaches our ears. Everything happens as though, by a miraculous favor, our very senses themselves had been made aware that silence is not the absence of sounds, but something infinitely more real than sounds, and the center of a harmony more perfect than anything which a combination of sounds can produce. Furthermore there are degrees of silence. There is a silence in the beauty of the universe which is like a noise when compared with the silence of God.

God is, moreover, our real neighbor. The term of person

can only be rightly applied to God, and this is also true of the term impersonal. God is he who bends over us, afflicted as we are, and reduced to the state of being nothing but a fragment of inert and bleeding flesh. Yet at the same time he is in some sort the victim of misfortune as well, the victim who appears to us as an inanimate body, incapable of thought, this nameless victim of whom nothing is known. The inanimate body is this created universe. The love we owe to God, this love that would be our crowning perfection if we were able to attain to it, is the divine model both of gratitude and compassion.

God is also the perfect friend. So that there should be between him and us, bridging the infinite distance, something in the way of equality, he has chosen to place an absolute quality in his creatures, the absolute liberty of consent, which leaves us free to follow or swerve from the God-ward direction he has communicated to our souls. He has also extended our possibilities of error and falsehood so as to leave us the faculty of exercising a spurious rule in imagination, not only over the universe and the human race, but also over God himself, in so far as we do not know how to use his name aright. He has given us this faculty of infinite illusion so that we should have the power to renounce it out of love.

In fact, contact with God is the true sacrament.

We can, however, be almost certain that those whose love of God has caused the disappearance of the pure loves belonging to our life here below are no true friends of God.

Our neighbor, our friends, religious ceremonies, and the beauty of the world do not fall to the level of unrealities after the soul has had direct contact with God. On the contrary, it is only then that these things become real. Previously they were half dreams. Previously they had no reality.

Concerning the Our Father

Πάτηρ ἡμῶν ὁ ἐν τοῖς οὐρανοῖς
"Our Father which art in Heaven."

He is our Father. There is nothing real in us which does not come from him. We belong to him. He loves us, since he loves himself and we are his. Nevertheless he is our Father who is in heaven—not elsewhere. If we think to have a Father here below it is not he, it is a false God. We cannot take a single step toward him. We do not walk vertically. We can only turn our eyes toward him. We do not have to search for him, we only have to change the direction in which we are looking. It is for him to search for us. We must be happy in the knowledge that he is infinitely beyond our reach. Thus we can be certain that the evil in us, even if it overwhelms our whole being, in no way sullies the divine purity, bliss, and perfection.

Ἁγιασθήτω τὸ ὄνομά σου
"Hallowed be thy Name."

God alone has the power to name himself. His name is unpronounceable for human lips. His name is his word. It is the Word of God. The name of any being is an intermediary between the human spirit and that being; it is the only means by which the human spirit can conceive something about a being that is absent. God is absent. He is in heaven. Man's only possibility of gaining access to him is through his name. It is the Mediator. Man has access to this name, although it also is transcendent. It shines in the beauty and order of the world and it shines in the interior light of the human soul. This name is holiness itself; there is no holiness outside it; it does not therefore have to be hallowed. In asking for its hallowing we are asking for something that exists eternally, with full and complete reality, so that we can neither increase nor diminish it, even by an infinitesimal fraction. To ask for that which exists, that which exists really, infallibly, eternally, quite independently of our prayer, that is the perfect petition. We cannot prevent ourselves from desiring; we are made of desire; but the desire that nails us down to what is imaginary, temporal, selfish, can, if we make it pass wholly into this petition, become a lever to tear us from the imaginary into the real and from time into eternity, to lift us right out of the prison of self.

ἐλθάτω ἡ βασιλεία σου

"Thy Kingdom Come."

This concerns something to be achieved, something not yet here. The Kingdom of God means the complete filling of the entire soul of intelligent creatures with the Holy Spirit. The Spirit bloweth where he listeth? We can only invite him. We must not even try to invite him in a definite and special way to visit us or anyone else in particular, or even everybody in general; we must just invite him purely and simply, so that our thought of him is an invitation, a longing cry. It is as when one is in extreme thirst, ill with thirst; then one no longer thinks of the act of drinking in relation to oneself, or even of the act of drinking in a general way. One merely thinks of water, actual water itself, but the image of water is like a cry from our whole being.

γενηθήτω τὸ θέλημά σου

"Thy will be done."

We are only absolutely, infallibly certain of the will of God concerning the past. Everything that has happened, whatever it may be, is in accordance with the will of the almighty Father. That is implied by the notion of almighty power. The future also, whatever it may contain, once it has come about, will have come about in conformity with the will of God. We can neither add to nor take from this conformity. In this clause, therefore, after an upsurging of our desire toward the possible, we are once again asking for that which is. Here, however, we are not concerned with an eternal reality such as the holiness of the Word, but with what happens in the time order. Nevertheless we are asking for the infallible and eternal conformity of everything in time with the will of God. After having, in our first petition, torn our desire away from time in order to fix it upon eternity, thereby transforming it, we return to this desire which has itself become in some measure eternal, in order to apply it once more to time. Whereupon our desire pierces through time to find eternity behind it. That is what comes about when we know how to make every accomplished fact, whatever it may be, an object of desire. We have here quite a different thing from resignation. Even the word acceptance is too weak. We have to desire that everything that has happened should have happened, and nothing else. We have to do so, not because what has happened is good in our eyes, but because God has permitted it, and because the obedience of the course of events to God is in itself an absolute good.

ὡς ἐν οὐρανῷ καὶ ἐπὶ γῆς

"On earth as it is in heaven."

The association of our desire with the almighty will of God should be extended to spiritual things. Our own spiritual ascents and falls, and those of the beings we love, have to do with the other world, but they are also events that take place here below, in time. On that account they are details in the immense sea of events and are tossed about with the ocean in a way conforming to the will of God. Since our failures of the past have come about, we have to desire that they should have come about. We have to extend this desire into the future, for the day when it will have become the past. It is a necessary correction of the petition that the kingdom of God should come. We have to cast aside all other desires for the sake of our desire for eternal life, but we should desire eternal life itself with renunciation. We must not even become attached to detachment. Attachment to salvation is even more dangerous than the others. We have to think of eternal life as one thinks of water when dying of thirst, and yet at the same time we have to desire that we and our loved ones should be eternally deprived of this water rather than receive it in abundance in spite of God's will, if such a thing were conceivable.

The three foregoing petitions are related to the three Persons of the Trinity, the Son, the Spirit, and the Father, and also to the three divisions of time, the present, the future, and the past. The three petitions that follow have a more direct bearing on the three divisions of time, and take them in a different order—present, past, and future.

Τὸν ἄρτον ἡμῶν τὸν ἐπιούσιον δὸς ἡμῖν σήμερον

"Give us this day our daily bread"—the bread which is supernatural.*

Christ is our bread. We can only ask to have him now. Actually he is always there at the door of our souls, wanting to enter in, though he does not force our consent. If we agree to his entry, he enters; directly we cease to want him, he is gone. We cannot bind our will today for tomorrow; we cannot make a pact with him that tomorrow he will be within us, even in spite of ourselves. Our consent to his presence is the same as his presence. Consent is an act; it can only be actual, that is to say in the present. We have not been given a will that can be applied to the future. Everything not effective in our will is imaginary. The effective part of the will has its effect at once; its effectiveness cannot be separated from itself. The effective part of the will is not effort, which is directed toward the future. It is consent; it is the "yes" of marriage. A "yes" pronounced within the present moment and for the present moment,

* Genesis 6:5.

but spoken as an eternal word, for it is consent to the union of Christ with the eternal part of our soul.

Bread is a necessity for us. We are beings who continually draw our energy from outside, for as we receive it we use it up in effort. If our energy is not daily renewed, we become feeble and incapable of movement. Besides actual food, in the literal sense of the word, all incentives are sources of energy for us. Money, ambition, consideration, decorations, celebrity, power, our loved ones, everything that puts into us the capacity for action is like bread. If anyone of these attachments penetrates deeply enough into us to reach the vital roots of our carnal existence, its loss may break us and even cause our death. That is called dying of love. It is like dying of hunger. All these objects of attachment go together with food, in the ordinary sense of the word, to make up the daily bread of this world. It depends entirely on circumstances whether we have it or not. We should ask nothing with regard to circumstances unless it be that they may conform to the will of God. We should not ask for earthly bread.

There is a transcendent energy whose source is in heaven, and this flows into us as soon as we wish for it. It is a real energy; it performs actions through the agency of our souls and of our bodies.

We should ask for this food. At the moment of asking, and by the very fact that we ask for it, we know that God will give it to us. We ought not to be able to bear to go without it for a single day, for when our actions only depend on earthly energies, subject to the necessity of this world, we are incapable of thinking and doing anything but evil. God saw "that the misdeeds of man were multiplied on the earth and that all the thoughts of his heart were continually bent upon evil." The necessity that drives us toward evil governs everything in us except the energy from on high at the moment when it comes into us. We cannot store it.

καὶ ἄφες ἡμῖν τὰ, ὀφειλήματα ἡμῶν, ὡς καὶ ἡμεῖς ἀφήκαμεν τοῖς ὀφειλέταις ἡμῶν

"And forgive us our debts, as we also forgive our debtors."

At the moment of saying these words we must have already remitted everything that is owing to us. This not only includes reparation for any wrongs we think we have suffered, but also gratitude for the good we think we have done, and it applies in a quite general way to all we expect from people and things, to all we consider as our due and without which we should feel ourselves to have been frustrated. All these are the rights that we think the past has given us over the future. First there is the right to a certain permanence. When we have enjoyed something for a long time, we think that it is ours and that we are entitled to expect fate to let us go on enjoying it. Then there is the right to a compensation for every effort whatever its nature, be it work, suffering, or desire. Every time that we put forth some effort and the equivalent of this effort does not come back to us in the form of some visible fruit, we have a sense of false balance and emptiness which makes us think that we have been cheated. The effort of suffering from some offense causes us to expect the punishment or apologies of the offender, the effort of doing good makes us expect the gratitude of the person we have helped, but these are only particular cases of a universal law of the soul. Every time we give anything out we have an absolute need that at least the equivalents should come into us, and because we need this we think we have a right to it. Our debtors comprise all beings and all things; they are the entire universe. We think we have claims everywhere. In every claim we think we possess there is always the idea of an imaginary claim of the past on the future. That is the claim we have to renounce.

To have forgiven our debtors is to have renounced the whole of the past in a lump. It is to accept that the future should still be virgin and intact, strictly united to the past by bonds of which we are ignorant, but quite free from the bonds our imagination thought to impose upon it. It means that we accept the possibility that this will happen, and that it may happen to us in particular; it means that we are prepared for the future to render all our past life sterile and vain.

In renouncing at one stroke all the fruits of the past without exception, we can ask of God that our past sins may not bear their miserable fruits of evil and error. So long as we cling to the past, God himself cannot stop this horrible fruiting. We cannot hold on to the past without retaining our crimes, for we are unaware of what is most essentially bad in us.

The principal claim we think we have on the universe is that our personality should continue. This claim implies all the others. The instinct of self-preservation makes us feel this continuation to be a necessity, and we believe that a necessity is a right. We are like the beggar who said to Talleyrand: "Sir, I must live," and to whom Talleyrand replied, "I do not see the necessity for that." Our personality is entirely dependent on external circumstances which have unlimited power to crush it. But we would rather die than admit this. From our point of view the equilibrium of the world is a combination of circumstances so ordered that our personality remains intact and seems to belong to us. All the circumstances of the past that have wounded our personality appear to us to be disturbances of balance which should infallibly be made up for one day or another by phenomena having a contrary effect. We live on the expectation of these compensations. The near approach of death is horrible chiefly because it forces the knowledge upon us that these compensations will never come.

To remit debts is to renounce our own personality. It means renouncing everything that goes to make up our ego, without any exception. It means knowing that in the ego there is nothing whatever, no psychological element, that external circumstances could not do away with. It means accepting that truth. It means being happy that things should be so.

The words "Thy will be done" imply this acceptance, if we say them with all our soul. That is why we can say a few moments later: "We forgive our debtors."

The forgiveness of debts is spiritual poverty, spiritual nakedness, death. If we accept death completely, we can ask God to make us live again, purified from the evil in us.

For to ask him to forgive us our debts is to ask him to wipe out the evil in us. Pardon is purification. God himself has not the power to forgive the evil in us while it remains there. God will have forgiven our debts when he has brought us to the state of perfection.

Until then God forgives our debts partially in the same measure as we forgive our debtors.

καὶ μὴ εἰσενέγκῃς ἡμᾶς εἰς πειρασμόν, ἀλλὰ ῥῦσαι ἡμᾶς ἀπὸ τοῦ πονηροῦ

"And lead us not into temptation, but deliver us from evil."

The only temptation for man is to be abandoned to his own resources in the presence of evil. His nothingness is then proved experimentally. Although the soul has received supernatural bread at the moment when it asked for it, its joy is mixed with fear because it could only ask for it for the present. The future is still to be feared. The soul has not the right to ask for bread for the morrow, but it expresses its fear in the form of a supplication. It finishes with that. The prayer began with the word "Father," it ends with the word "evil." We must go from confidence to fear. Confidence alone can give us strength enough not to fall as a result of fear. After having contemplated the name, the kingdom, and the will of God, after having received the supernatural bread and having been purified from evil, the soul is ready for that true humility which crowns all virtues. Humility consists of knowing that in this world the whole soul, not only what we term the ego in its totality, but also the supernatural part of the soul, which is God present in it, is subject to time and to the vicissitudes of change. There must be absolute acceptance of the possibility that everything natural in us should be destroyed. But we must simultaneously accept and repudiate the possibility that the supernatural part of the soul should disappear. It must be accepted as an event that would come about only in conformity with the will of God. It must be repudiated as being something utterly horrible. We must be afraid of it, but our fear must be as it were the completion of confidence.

The six petitions correspond with each other in pairs. The bread which is transcendent is the same thing as the divine name. It is what brings about the contact of man with God. The kingdom of God is the same thing as his protection stretched over us against temptation; to protect is the function of royalty. Forgiving our debtors their debts is the same thing as the total acceptance of the will of God. The difference is that in the first three petitions the attention is fixed solely on God. In the three last, we turn our attention back to ourselves in order to compel ourselves to make these petitions a real and not an imaginary act.

In the first half of the prayer, we begin with acceptance. Then we allow ourselves a desire. Then we correct it by coming back to acceptance. In the second half, the order is changed; we finish by expressing desire. Only desire has now become negative; it is expressed as a fear; therefore it corresponds to the highest degree of humility and that is a fitting way to end.

The Our Father contains all possible petitions; we cannot conceive of any prayer not already contained in it. It is to prayer what Christ is to humanity. It is impossible to say it once through, giving the fullest possible attention to each word, without a change, infinitesimal perhaps but real, taking place in the soul.